Finding Freedom in a Binding World

Lisa Buffaloe

Finding Freedom in a Binding World
Copyright 2025 Lisa Brewer Buffaloe
John 15:11 Publications
All rights reserved.

Unless with the author's permission, no part of this book may be reproduced or transmitted in any way, form, or by any means, electronic or mechanical, including photocopying, recording, or using any information storage and retrieval system, except for brief quotations in printed or online reviews.

The author prohibits any entity from using this publication to train AI technologies to generate text, including, without limitation, technologies capable of generating works in the same style or genre as this publication.

Visit the author's website at https://lisabuffaloe.com.

Cover Design: Lisa Buffaloe (Cityscape photo by Toshiharu Watanabe)

ISBN: 978-1-957715-55-1 (eBook)
ISBN: 978-1-957715-56-8 (Paperback)
ISBN: 978-1-957715-57-5 (Hardcover)

Table of Contents

TABLE OF CONTENTS III

FINDING FREEDOM IN A BINDING WORLD 1

SOUL CARE 10
    SOUL SCRUB 14
    FORGIVEN AND FORGIVING 19
    LET THE PAST SLEEP 23

TAMING THOUGHTS AND RIDDING WORRIES 27
    TAKING BACK AIR RIGHTS 33
    WORD WATCH 36
    THE CALM CENTER 39

THE CHALLENGING ADVENTURE 42
    BRAVE SUFFERING 53
    BEYOND THE WOUND 59
    GLORY BEYOND THE PAIN 62
    WHEN SUFFERING CONTINUES 67
    TENDER BOUNDARIES 72
    PRAISE POWER 79

MOVING FORWARD 87
    GUARD YOUR HEART AND STRENGTHEN THE CORE 97
    WAIT WELL 101
    LIVE IN THE MOMENT 108
    GLOW AND SHINE 112
    BE AN ENCOURAGER 115
    SHARE THE GOOD NEWS 118

YOU'LL GET SAFELY THROUGH 122
    THE JOYFUL END 124
    ONE LAST NOTE 128

ABOUT THE AUTHOR 129

ACKNOWLEDGMENTS 131

BIBLE CREDITS AND BIBLIOGRAPHY 132

Finding freedom in a binding world

Ever heard of the watermelon challenge? The idea is to place rubber bands, one by one, around the middle of a watermelon. As the tension builds, the pressure continues to mount until the watermelon explodes.

The result is very, very, very messy.

Have you felt like that watermelon, as life binds, placing pressure day after day and moment by moment? Health issues, family issues, money issues, city, local, state, country, and world issues squeeze until you're about to explode.

Life can pick us apart piece by piece until we can't find peace.

When the world has tilted off its axis and is flying out of control, what do we do when the answers don't come, the waiting doesn't end, and the suffering doesn't stop?

We're bound up in our messed-up world with frustration, fear, concerns, depression, and endless worries.

How can we find freedom in a world that binds?

The Bible is God's answer book, His love letter to the world. Within the Old and New Testaments lies a wealth of information that brings answers, comfort, wisdom, encouragement, knowledge, inspiration, strength, and faith, all designed to help us unbind and live free, even in a binding world.

Early in the ministry of Jesus Christ, He read from the book of Isaiah, "The Spirit of the Lord is upon Me, because He anointed Me to bring good news to the poor. He has sent Me to proclaim release to captives, and recovery of sight to the blind, to set free those who are oppressed, to proclaim the favorable year of the Lord" (Luke 4:18, NASB).

It was for freedom that Christ set us free, and if the Son sets us free, we really will be free (Galatians 5:1, John 8:36).

How do we find the freedom Christ offers?

The notes for this book began in 2019 and grew to a massive computer file as I searched for answers, Bible verses, quotes, and encouragement for me and others. No matter what I tried, I couldn't figure out how to make the book "fit" into a proper size for a devotional or a chapter book; it almost seemed free-flowing and fluid.

Then I realized that's life. Life's journey constantly shifts, shaped by diverse events of varying lengths.

Therefore, I gathered information that I hope will serve as a source of inspiration and encouragement as we face the often unforeseen, seemingly chaotic, random, and unpleasant events that challenge our peace, hope, and dreams.

Drawing inspiration and timeless wisdom from the Bible, quotes, and stories of perseverance, each section will explore how God's promises and Jesus' teachings bring comfort, wisdom, and true freedom as we face a myriad of issues on our journey.

Join the journey to discover how you can live free in a world that binds.

Finding Freedom in a Binding World

As we start, let's establish one truth as a foundation.

The truth is God is compassionate, merciful, tender-hearted, loving, and caring. In God's presence is fullness of joy, and in His hand are pleasures forever (Psalm 16:11), and Jesus Christ brings full, complete, overflowing joy (John 15:11).

The magnitude of the love of God and the love of Jesus is more than we can imagine or conceive.

> Jesus "was the heart of God throbbing love out to man's heart. He was the face of God looking into man's face. He was the voice of God, soft and low, clear and distinct, speaking into man's ears. He was the hand of God, strong and tender, reaching down to take man by the hand and lead him back to the old tree of life, down by the river of water of life. He was the person of God wearing a human coat and human shoes, walking in freely among us so that we might get our tangled-up ideas about God and ourselves and about life untangled, straightened out. He was God wrapped up in human form, coming close so that we get acquainted with Him all over again. Man had grown deaf to the music of God's voice, blind to the beauty of His face, slow hearted to the pleading of His presence. We couldn't read His signature, plainly autographed by His own hand, on all of nature around us. But when Jesus came, men knew God by the feel of Him. He came in a new way, in a very homely close-up way and walked down our street, into our own doors, that we might be captivated by the beauty of His face, thrilled by the music of His voice, and enthralled by the beauty of His presence." ~ S. D. Gordon[1]

Take the most tender love you have ever known, the most

joyful, loving person, the most joyful moment of your life, and that is only a microscopic view of the love of God and the joy of Jesus Christ.

> "The more I know about God, the more I want to know about God. And as I begin to experience His love, I begin to see levels of His love that I did not notice before. I begin to see that God's love is bigger than anything I could ever imagine. As I begin to see how big this love of God is, I begin to experience that love in my own life." ~ A. W. Tozer[2]

The remarkable reality is that God's love, the love of Jesus, is available to you.

Know what else is amazing? God personally and lovingly created you.

> "Before we existed in this world, we existed in His heart."
> ~ Charles Spurgeon

God created your inmost being and knit you together in your mother's womb. God's thoughts about you are so vast that they would outnumber the grains of sand. He knows the number of hairs on your head, and your name is engraved on the palms of His hands (Psalm 139:13, 17-18, Luke 12:7, Isaiah 49:16).

You are God's unique creation for unique purposes. No one is like you, no one can replace you, and no one fills God's heart like you.

God is intimately acquainted with you, thinks constantly about you, and rejoices and sings over you while you sleep. God watches over you and doesn't slumber or sleep. (Jeremiah 31:3, Psalm 139:17-18, Psalm 121:1-4, Zephaniah 3:17).

Nothing is ordinary about how you were created. God made you extraordinary. Just consider: an average heart beats 80 times per minute, which means your heart beats about 4,800 times per hour and 115,200 times per day. If you took all the blood vessels out of the average adult, they would be close to 100,000 miles long.

Truly, you are fearfully and wonderfully made (Psalm 139:14).

> "Before you were born, you existed in the mind of God. He decided that the world needed you at a certain time—that there is something for you to do that is different from what any other person will do. Everything God made has its own peculiar identity. There are billions of blades of grass, but no two are alike. No two snowflakes have ever been identical. No person who ever existed is exactly like you. Even the print of your little finger is separate and distinct. It should lift you to a new realization of importance to know that of all the billions of people the earth has known, there is only one of you." ~ Charles L. Allen[3]

God's love is eternal, and with unwavering devotion, He beckons you to come closer.

When our son was a toddler, he would run to the door to greet his daddy when he returned home. Thinking back, I still can hear the pitter-patter of his little feet on the floor, the swish of his diaper, and the squeal of joy when my husband opened the door. Dennis would stoop to meet Scott, envelop him in his arms, and bring him to his chest.

God's arms are open wide to welcome *you* into His love.

Through God's great love and mercy, through the kindness and sacrifice, death, and resurrection of His Son, Jesus Christ, is an amazing, grace-filled, power-filled gift for all who believe.

Jesus stands at the door of your heart and knocks.

Should you open, accept Jesus as Lord and Savior, He will come in, and in His Father's house, an amazing, forever home is prepared just for you. (Revelation 3:20, John 14:2-3).

By giving your heart to Jesus, you begin to truly know God, just as He has always known and loved you.

> "Knowing God is to understand our reason for existence—our purpose in life." ~ A. W. Tozer[4]

Your salvation is personal, and God's care is personal.

Jesus has intimate knowledge of his followers, and they know Him in return. His sheep hear His voice, and they follow Him. Those who love God are known by God. (John 10:14, John 10:27).

> "The design of God in the creation of men has been to associate to himself living beings, to whom he could communicate himself."
> ~ Madam Guyon[5]

"Mom!" A child's voice echoed from beyond the open door.

Twenty heads jerked to attention. However, only the mother rose to her feet and followed the sound of her child's voice.

When I was young, my mother's beautiful soprano voice reverberated in our home as she sang hymns. I knew her voice.

While playing outside as children, my dad used a whistle to call us to return. We knew his whistle anywhere, and the sound of his voice called us safely home.

God also calls to you.

Jesus knew His Father's voice and listened for His guidance and direction. God offers through Christ the same beautiful relationship.

> "If God did not mean to hear us, He would not bid us pray."
> ~ Charles Spurgeon

Throughout the Bible are recorded instances of people hearing God's voice — Adam, Eve, Job, Noah, Abraham, Jacob, Moses, Aaron, Elijah, Joshua, Gideon, Samuel, David, and the list goes on and on.

God speaks through His Holy Spirit, His Word, and through creation. God speaks through gifted Bible teachers, through whatever means God chooses. He even used a donkey.

> "The greatest privilege God gives to you is the freedom to approach Him at any time. You are not only authorized to speak to Him; you are invited. You are not only permitted; you are expected. God waits for you to communicate with Him. You have instant, direct access to God. God loves mankind so much, and in a very special sense His children, that He has made Himself available to you at all times." ~ Wesley L. Duewel

When Jesus Christ lives within you, you are a child of God; therefore, as His child, you hear your Heavenly Father. God's loving voice calls to you through His Son.

Prayer is a divine invitation to meet with the Divine.

> "There is no greater joy on earth or in heaven than communion with God, and prayer in the name of Jesus brings us into communion with Him. The psalmist was surely not speaking only of future blessedness, but also of present blessedness when he said, 'In Your presence is fullness of joy' (Psalm 16:11 NKJV). O, the unutterable joy of those moments when in our prayers we really press into the presence of God!" ~ R. A. Torrey

God is calling for you to meet with Him, drawing you close so that your soul can find His rest, peace, guidance, and joy.

The Divine Invitation is addressed to you.

> "If we allow the thought of Jesus Christ to delight and overawe our hearts, He will become more to us than our nearest friend."
> - Alexander Whyte

God invites, Call to Me, and I will answer you, and I will tell you great and mighty things, which you do not know (Jeremiah 33:3).

> "God hears wishes, heart-longings, soul hungerings, and thirstings. The things we cannot say in speech of the lips, we may ask God to take from our heart's speech. Our truest praying is that which we cannot express in any words, our heart's unutterable longings, when we sit at God's feet and look into his face and do not speak at all but let our hearts talk." ~ J. R. Miller[6]

Come to Me, Jesus beckons, and I will cause you to rest. I will ease and relieve and refresh your souls. You will find rest (relief and ease and refreshment and recreation and blessed quiet) for your souls (Matthew 11:28-29). Will you come?

> "Thou hast made us for Thyself, O Lord, and our heart is restless until it finds its rest in Thee." ~ St. Augustine

The invitation of God leads to the adventure of God.

> "Fling wide, then, the portals of your soul. He will come with that love which you long to feel; he will come with that joy into which you cannot work your poor, depressed spirit; he will bring the peace which now you have not. Only open the door to him, drive out his enemies, give him the keys of your heart, and he will dwell there forever. Oh, wondrous love, that brings such a guest to dwell in such a heart! The whole of Christ, in His adorable character as the Son of God, is by Himself made over to us most richly to enjoy. His wisdom is our direction, his knowledge our instruction, his power our protection, his justice our surety, his love our comfort, his mercy our solace, and his immutability our trust. He makes no reserve, but opens the recesses of the Mount of God and bids us dig in its mines for the hidden treasures."
> ~ Charles Spurgeon[7]

The most amazing freedom is found in never forgetting that the God of love loves you.

> "No matter what your circumstances are, God's love never changes. The cross, Jesus Christ's death, and resurrection are God's final, total, and complete expression of His love for you. Never allow your heart to question God's love. Settle it on the front end of your desire to know Him and experience Him. He loves you. He created you for a love relationship. He has been pursuing you in that love relationship." ~ Henry and Richard Blackaby, Claude King[8]

Soul care

> "What matters most, what marks your existence, the really deep reason why human life matters so much, is because of this tiny, fragile, vulnerable, precious thing about you called your soul. You are not just a self; you are a soul. You are a soul made by God, made for God, and made to need God, made to run on God."
> ~ Dallas Willard [9]

In his book *The Rest of God*, Mark Buchanan wrote that he grew up in an area where winters were impossibly cold and could be deadly for anyone or any animal left outside for too long.

The family cats were kept inside, and when the afternoon sun tipped into their living room, they would emerge from wherever they had been in the house "to curl up or sprawl out in the warm pools of light. They lay in utter contentment, with almost boneless stillness." His impression was that the "cats were emptying themselves and filling themselves all at once." The rest of God is "an invitation, at one and the same time, to empty yourself and fill yourself."[10]

Your soul needs to rest with the One who made your soul.

We need a safe place where our souls can relax, let go of the

Finding Freedom in a Binding World

world's worries, and breathe deep of God's healing, restorative love.

God is the home for our hearts, and in God's presence is fullness of joy, and in His right hand, there are pleasures forever (Psalm 16:11).

God invites, "Be still and know that I am God."

Be still in Hebrew means to sink down, let drop, be quiet, or relax. Being still and knowing God is an invitation, a discovery, an offer of fellowship with our loving Creator. In the stillness, we hear, rest, learn, and discover who we are and Whose we are.

> "Solitude with God repairs the damage done by the fret and noise of the clamor of the world." ~ Oswald Chambers

Think about the most breathtaking natural scenery you've ever encountered. Picture that place, that perfect place. Perhaps a sunset bathed in bright colors, a majestic mountain range, a white sandy beach with turquoise water, or the stars twinkling at midnight.

What makes your heart smile?

Picture Jesus sitting next to you, smiling and loving you. The past, present, and future disappear in the light of His presence.

God is the One who restores souls.

> "For the soul to be well, it needs to be with God. This is sustaining grace—grace that replenishes and enables the soul to rest. A soul centered in God always knows it has a heavenly Father who will hold its anxiety, fear, and pain." ~ John Ortberg[11]

Christ holds out His loving, nail-scarred hand. Come to Me, and I will give you rest. Take My yoke upon you and learn of Me, for I am gentle (meek) and humble (lowly) in heart, and you will find rest (relief and ease and refreshment and recreation and blessed quiet) for your souls, (Matthew 11:28-29, AMPC)

For most of my life, taking a yoke upon me (even if it is easy) didn't sound very restful.

I visualized a large ox yoked with a smaller one. The bigger animal shouldered the larger burden, while the smaller one toiled, attempting to keep up and contribute.

However, the Lord blessed me with a visual that makes more sense. Jesus Christ, the Son of God, the Prince of Peace, stands tall with the yoke across His mighty shoulders.

Standing beside Him, I'm tiny against His powerful presence. The cords that bind me to His yoke drift down, light and easy. My feet barely touch the ground as Jesus moves forward. I'm swinging, swaying, rejoicing to be led by Him.

Jesus carries the burdens.

He shoulders every hardship and difficulty. The only time the yoke is heavy is when we pull ahead or strain to maneuver and do things our own way.

> "True rest to the mind of the child of God is rest on the wing, rest in motion, rest in service, not rest with the yoke off, but with the yoke on." ~ Charles Spurgeon

Let's look again at what Jesus shared in Matthew, this time from the MSG version. "Come to me. Get away with me, and you'll recover your life. I'll show you how to take a real rest. Walk with me and work with me—watch how I do it. Learn the unforced rhythms of grace. I won't lay anything heavy or ill-fitting on you. Keep company with me, and you'll learn to live freely and lightly." (Matthew 11:28-30, MSG)

Doesn't that sound wonderful? Keep company with Jesus. Walk with Him, abide, dwell, remain, live and move, and have your being in God's presence in His unforced rhythms of grace.

Various translations of that passage in Matthew read Jesus said Come to Him and for us to learn of Him, or learn from Him. He invites us — Come to Me, learn from Me, learn Me.

Studying Jesus, learning Jesus, learning of Jesus, and learning from Jesus is the key. Jesus said, If you've seen Me, you've seen the Father. As we spend time with Jesus — reading about Him and learning about Him — we come to know the Father.

As far as we know, during His time in ministry, Jesus didn't run anywhere. Christ didn't hurry from place to place. He didn't rent chariots or ride horses to get somewhere faster.

Jesus traveled on foot, by boat, and even miraculously walked on water during a terrible storm. Jesus spent time with His Father in prayer and did what the Father told Him to do.

> "Fully dependent on God, Jesus never seemed to rush from one place to another. He was purposeful rather than driven, available rather than busy, touchable rather than distant. Because He was led by the Holy Spirit, Jesus saw everything and everyone as part of God's will for His life. And because he trusted that the Father had everything under control, His life was marked by a beautiful peace. Imagine what our lives would be like if we did the same."
> ~ Joanna Weaver[12]

The rest God offers is more than being immobile.

There is a soul rest, a soul at rest in the presence of God — a soul that has found home regardless of the body's physical location, health, inactivity, or activity.

> "I don't really want more time; I just want enough time. Time to breathe deep and time to see real and time to laugh long, time to give You glory and rest deep and sing joy. I just want time to do my one life well. Life at its fullest is this sensitive, detonating sphere — and it can be carried only in the hands of the unhurried and reverential — a bubble held in awe." ~ Ann Voskamp[13]

Soul scrub

We all need spiritual cleansing. We've all sinned (Romans 3:23).

"Every part of the world bears testimony to the fact that sin is the universal disease of mankind." ~ J. C. Ryle

Several years ago, a TV commercial for a spot-cleaning product was broadcast. A young job applicant sat across the desk from a company executive. The executive's attention was entirely consumed by the prominent stain on the young man's shirt.

In the same way, sin blocks our communication and separates us from our holy God.

Sin always has consequences. The Lord will not hear us if we harbor sin in our hearts (Psalm 66:18). Isaiah 59:2 reminds us that your wrongdoings have caused a separation between you and your God, and your sins have hidden His face from you so that He does not hear.

It's crucial to avoid dismissing our sins or treating them as if they're not a problem. When God tells people to repent of their sins, He allows the opportunity for cleansing and the restoration of a right relationship with God.

My ear throbbed and ached, and relief was nowhere to be found. The doctor prescribed an antibiotic, yet the pain continued. My pain tolerance is extremely high, and I was sure the inside of my ear was bleeding profusely as the eardrum vibrated with agony.

Worst. Ear. Infection. Ever!

I mentioned the problem to a friend, and she shared a time

when acid reflux backed up into her ear canals, causing her ears to become infected. What? I didn't even know that could happen.

Acid reflux can be brought on by eating and then lying down soon after. To avoid digestive fluids from entering your esophagus, throat, or possibly your ear canal, it's important to remain upright.

How many people are nibbling away on sin, lying down in sin, thinking no harm will come?

Sin is like acid reflux, eating away, infecting, destroying, and causing agony.

No sin is just a "little" sin; every sin comes with a negative consequence.

> "You have to slay sin, or your sin will slay you."
> ~ Charles Spurgeon

David understood that. He wrote, "When I kept silent about my sin, my body wasted away through my groaning all day long," (Psalm 32:3, NASB).

However, there is good news. Christ's grace and love forgives the sins of those who seek His mercy.

Got sin? Jesus is the cure and the relief. He went to the cross in our place, taking all our sins on His innocent shoulders. Christ forgives and grants new life.

God loves you; Christ loves you so much that Christ died for you while you were *still* a sinner.

> "When God looks at humanity and sees the depravity and the sin, certainly there is pain, and certainly there are tears. That is why God sent His Son, so that we might be able to receive the emotional love that He has for us—and this love cannot be compromised, because nothing can overcome the power and passion of our God." ~ A. W. Tozer[14]

When you were spiritually dead because of your sins and because you were not free from the power of your sinful self, God made you alive with Christ, and forgave all your sins. For He rescued you from the domain of darkness, and transferred you to the kingdom of His beloved Son, in whom you have redemption, the forgiveness of sins (Colossians 2:13, Colossians 1:13-14).

> "My sins needed something more than disinfecting; they needed incinerating. In the flames of Calvary, that is what happened. Now I am free." ~ Selwyn Hughes

Before Jesus's crucifixion, Peter denied Christ three times. However, Peter later shared with others (many of whom had earlier demanded Jesus be crucified) to "repent and turn back, so that your sins may be wiped out, that seasons of refreshing may come from the presence of the Lord."

The Amplified version adds restoring you like a cool wind on a hot day.

I love these verses because Peter understood that there is nothing more refreshing than a loving, forgiving Savior.

That refreshing, cleansing through God's amazing grace is also available for you.

Never be afraid to come to God or return home to God. God is good, ready to forgive, abundant in lovingkindness, and rich in mercy.

God's mercies are new every morning and never end.

Come to God's throne of grace. If you confess your sins, God is faithful and righteous to forgive and cleanse you from all unrighteousness. He sweeps away your sins like a cloud and scatters your offenses like the morning mist.

Return to Me, God invites, for I have paid the price to set you free. And when you do, God removes your sins as far as the East is from the West.

> When Christ comes into my life, God looks at me and does not see my past; all He sees is that delightful reflection of His Son, the Lord Jesus Christ." ~ A. W. Tozer[15]

The Lord blesses with forgiveness with a reminder to go and sin no more (John 8:11).

> "The man may have been guilty of an atrocious sin, but if he comes to Christ, he shall never be driven away. To that atrocious sin, he may have added many others, but if he comes to Jesus, he shall not be cast out. He may have made himself as dark as hell; yet the Lord will not cast out the person who comes to Him. Be your character what it may, you shall not be turned away. Through Jesus Christ, if you but believe in Him, your whole past shall be rolled up and put away, as though it had never existed, and you shall be born again. Let us look into the beautiful face of Jesus and believe that He does indeed receive us; and if He receives us, we are received into the heart of God; we are received into eternal life; and eventually we shall be received into everlasting blessedness. Oh, the joy that is so absolutely certain!"
> ~ Charles Spurgeon

Often, we are aware of the sin in our lives. Please also ask God to reveal any concealed sins. Please don't give the devil more time to accuse you, beat you down, and keep you from a right relationship with God.

> "Sin hurts people and ruins relationships. But perhaps the greatest tragedy is what sin keeps us from—the grand adventure of a life lived with and for God." ~ Drew Dyck

For the amazing freedom of forgiveness, mercy, grace, cleansing, restoration, times of refreshing, joy, and celebration, come to your tender, compassionate God and go on the grand adventure of life.

Forgiven and forgiving

In the Old Testament, the Israelites offered sacrifices for their sins. That practice gave a reminder and a visual. The flames consumed the sacrifice of the sin that stood in the way of a relationship with a righteous and holy God. The smell, the smoke rising to Heaven, and the knowledge of releasing that sin had to be freeing.

In the same way, if something continues to trouble me, something I just can't seem to release, I'll write it down and take it to God in prayer, then, in a safe place, I'll burn the paper as a sacrifice.

If there are things you have had trouble releasing — things you have done or things others have done to you—if you would be willing, write those things down. Not to relive the pain, but to write them to God.

> "If you do not grieve, you'll be stuck holding onto old things in your heart. Instead, do as Paul did when he 'considered everything a loss' (Phil. 3:8). Talk about the past. Acknowledge it. Grieve over it, as God designed. (he gave you tear ducts for a reason.) Then let it go. Lose it. This death opens the door for a resurrection. Do not fear mourning and pay no attention to anyone who tells you that mourning the past is unbiblical. 'Blessed are those who mourn, for they shall be comforted' (Matt. 5:4)." ~ Dr. Henry Cloud[16]

What stays in the darkness grows darker.

Write all that happened, everything bothering you, everything you can't forgive, and anything that continues to torment you, and take them to God. Read aloud, cry, wail, and tell God exactly how you feel about what happened, how you feel about everything.

Take it to God.

> "Adversity invites us to mourn. Such grieving demands a level of vulnerability that can make us want to run, hide, and avoid the outpouring. When done well, the tears of mourning become a river that washes away our pain, a holy stream carrying us toward healing, wholeness, and joy." ~ Margaret Feinberg[17]

Grieve, talk to God, ask Him to forgive you, and ask Him to help you forgive. Release what happened, and lay it at His feet. Then, if you have a safe place, burn those pages. Burn them.

As the fire consumes your written words, smell and watch the smoke as it rises to Heaven. Burn them. As the edges of the papers curl, the words disintegrate, and you will have a visual of your freedom.

When the enemy taunts you with past mistakes, or the reminder of past sin, or past burdens, you'll have the memory of the visual of those items given to God, where everything falls under His justice, righteousness, and grace.

We're forgiven; we must also forgive.

> "Though forgiveness isn't easy, it's incredibly important. For an offended heart not only shuts out people, it shuts out God."
> ~ Joanna Weaver[18]

Jesus prayed, "Forgive us for our sins, just as we have forgiven those who sinned against us."

Then He added, "If you forgive others for their sins, your Father in heaven will also forgive you for your sins. But if you don't forgive others, your Father in heaven will not forgive your sins,"

(Matthew 6:12, 14-15, NCV).

Please don't allow the devil to keep you locked in unforgiveness and bitterness.

> "The bitter individual overlooks the fact that forgiveness is a gift not only for the offender but also for the offended. Forgiveness begins the work of liberating us from the pain and poison of the incident that wounded us." ~ Rob Currie[19]

Forgive others <u>so you can be free</u>.

> "Forgiveness doesn't erase the ache. It doesn't fill the empty chair at the table or silence the echo of a voice we'll never hear again. But I know this: forgiveness is freedom. And I know it because I've lived it." Janet's nineteen-year-old son, Joe, had been murdered, and yet the man who took Joe's life was acquitted. The man who killed her son walked out free. We walked out broken. In the weeks that followed, I wept. I questioned. I prayed. And in the silence of my grief, I felt God's peace wash over me. It didn't make sense. But it made me whole. And it gave me the courage to do the one thing I never thought I could do: Forgive the man who killed my Joe. Here's what I've learned on this sacred road: When you forgive, you don't rewrite the past—you step into God's purpose. When you forgive, you don't grow bitter—you grow better. When you forgive, you don't excuse the hurt—you release its hold on your life. And when you forgive, you trade anger for peace... and begin again. Forgiveness didn't change what happened. But it changed me. So I ask you, from one heart to another—Are you ready to lay the weight down? Are you ready to walk in the freedom forgiveness brings?" ~ Janet Perez Eckles[20]

Forgiving others does not question the reality of your wounds, the level of your pain, or that you have been sinned against.

> "Forgiveness means taking someone off your hook and placing him or her on God's hook." ~ Sharon Jaynes[21]

Forgiveness is not what you do for others; forgiving others is a gift for you. Forgiving others frees you and restores the relationship with God.

Forgive and live free.

Let the past sleep

Making his way to the end zone, the athlete tucked the football under his arm and outran the other players on the field. He made a quick glance over his shoulder to see how far his opponents were behind him.

His feet tangled, and he fell face-first only two yards from the goal line. That one glance caused him to stumble, and the game was lost.

How frequently is the past revisited?

The past condemns and torments with the "wish we had done that", the "should have done that", or the "wish we hadn't done that", or "wish that hadn't happened", which leaves us tangled and bound to the torments and condemnation of the past.

The enemy wants us to believe that we can't change, that God won't forgive, or redeem and restore our messy pasts.

Satan is a liar.

God truly is in the restoration business.

When we lived in Fort Worth, we often visited the Botanical Gardens. Nestled within are the Japanese Gardens, a tranquil retreat from the rush of the world. The garden's blend of Japanese maples, cherry trees, bamboo, bridges, waterfalls, and plants melds with the gentle, rolling terrain, making it seem as if the gardens have existed for hundreds of years.

We visited the gardens for years before learning that the land had been initially used as a trash dump, a watering hole for cattle, a squatter's camp, and then as a gravel pit to build the streets of old

Fort Worth.

When we lived in the Boise area, we often visited the Idaho Botanical Gardens, established on the site of old prison grounds.

Never would we have guessed that something as beautiful as those gardens could have come from such ugly beginnings.

How many have stood over the trash heap of a life, or a life considered too broken and chained, and declared that it would never be free and always be a trash heap?

> "God is all about redemption. His love for humanity runs deeper than the deepest recesses of our depravity. His love extends further than your past, higher than your disappointments, wider than your heart wounds, and deeper than a cavernous pit of depression. God's plan of redemption is for every person, no matter where you've been, no matter what you've been through, no matter what you've done." ~ Gwen Smith[22]

No matter how unworthy or broken you feel or how deep the sin, God's forgiveness and grace are freely offered. God sees beyond the brokenness, the squatters of sin, the prison of despair, and hopelessness.

We can trust Him to forgive, and when we do, He makes us new and recreates us into walking testaments of His grace and mercy.

> "It's not enough to know the promises of God; you've got to grab hold with all the firmness of the trapeze artist—release what is behind and take hold of what is ahead." ~ Sharon Jaynes[23]

God is always doing new things.

"Do not call to mind the former things, or ponder things of the past. Behold, I will do something new; now it will spring forth; will you not be aware of it? I will even make a roadway in the wilderness, rivers in the desert," (Isaiah 43:18-19, NASB).

> "Let the past sleep, but let it sleep on the bosom of Christ, and go out into the irresistible future with Him." ~ Oswald Chambers

Paul shared, forgetting what is behind, and reaching forward for what is before, I press toward the mark (Philippians 3:13).

Do you come from a family with a terrible reputation? Rahab was a prostitute. Her son Boaz married Ruth, who came from a godless, idol-worshiping nation. Yet they are listed in the genealogy of Jesus Christ.

Have you been taken from a good family and placed in a godless one? Look at the stories of Moses and Daniel.

Do your siblings hate you? Read about Joseph's family.

Have you been falsely accused and thrown in prison? Look again at Joseph's story.

Have you lied and put others in an unpleasant situation? Read the stories of Abraham and Jacob.

Have you murdered someone? Consider the stories of Moses and David.

Have you committed adultery? Look again at David's story.

Even those who lied and committed crimes were forgiven and given new opportunities to live Godly lives.

> "The Bible is filled with people just like you and me who failed miserably, wounded themselves and others, and were still met with divine mercy." ~ Gwen Smith[24]

David committed adultery, had an innocent man killed, yet when David repented of his sins, God forgave him. And what's even more amazing is that God called David a man after His own heart.

> David "had a black chapter of sin and failure in his life. But he spends no time in useless regret and morbid looking back."
> ~ Dr. Charles Allen

I love Dr. Allen's statement. I do not want to spend another moment with useless regret and morbid looking back.

The past can't be changed.

A prayer I pray is that God would help me forget what He wants me to forget and remember what He wants me to remember.

No matter how often events are replayed, and I wish things were different, the past cannot be changed. Yet, Jesus Christ offers forgiveness and freedom.

> "You can't go back and change the beginning, but you can start where you are and change the ending." ~ C.S. Lewis

No more looking behind. No more living in shame. Step forward in Christ's freedom.

> "God wants to remind you today that the same God who has dealt with every sin and wrong deed you've ever done has the ability to make you forget the negative and hurtful things in your life. The grace of God can overcome their power to haunt you."
> ~ Jim Cymbala[25]

Whatever you were in the past, whatever was done to you, whatever you did — Jesus washes you clean and restores what the enemy has stolen.

> "Christ doesn't want anyone living in the shadows of their past, but instead in the light of His future for them." ~ Tracie Miles

Taming thoughts and ridding worries

What is the best way to deal with racing, rampant thoughts, and the anxieties and worries that mess with our heads?

> "Worry is fear that has unpacked its bags and signed a long-term lease." ~ John Ortberg[26]

One night, I dreamed I was traveling with a friend. While she daintily carried a small overnight bag, I struggled to drag a bounty of large, overflowing suitcases. When I awakened, I realized the dream pointed out a bigger problem than packing for a trip.

Far too often, my "bags" are filled with worries over what did happen, what might happen, what others did, what others do and might do, along with concerns about family, life, and the world, worries about anything and everything, dragging and tangling my mind in a mangled mess.

Whatever is keeping me anxious reveals that I am not trusting God with that concern.

What if worries formed visible worrywarts?

Gasp!

There are days when worrywarts would cover me from head to

toe.

How much time is wasted worrying?

How frequently do our minds form nightmarish worst-case scenarios?

My husband and I sleep with our ceiling fan on full blast to keep the air moving and prevent me from going up in flames during hot flashes. One night, however, since the outside temperature was extremely frigid, we turned the fan to a lower speed.

I woke in the night and heard what sounded like scratching, or tiny feet, like mice feet, in the ceiling over my head. Not wanting to wake my husband, I lay there imagining all kinds of terrible things happening in our attic. Were mice building giant nests, eating the lumber and sheetrock, dancing mice discos, and destroying our house? My very fertile imagination created all sorts of nightmarish scenarios.

By morning, I was ready to get a flamethrower and take action. Fortunately, my husband was smart enough and kind enough to check the attic before I did anything rash. He found no problems, nor did he find an army of mice marching around the rafters.

I returned to our bedroom, turned on the ceiling fan, and waited.

Sure enough, the scratching sound started up again. Were the mice waiting to come out in the fan's cover noise?

Oh, man, they were a sneaky bunch!

Before I threw a smoke bomb up the attic stairs, I decided to turn the fan on high. And what do you know?

The noise went away. I turned the fan to the lower speed, and the scratching sound started again.

Then it hit me: the fan's vibration was the actual sound I was hearing. Sigh. I put away the smoke bomb and flamethrower and quietly walked away.

> "Worry is a cycle of inefficient thoughts whirling around a center of fear." ~ Corrie Ten Boom

Dwelling on anxieties only makes them grow more frightening and more worrisome.

However, when we fixate and focus on God, who is loving, all-powerful, merciful, kind, and compassionate, we are shielded from the enemy and protected from anxiety.

> "Worry is sin; a black, murderous, God-defying, Christ-rejecting sin; worry about anything, at any time whatever. We will never know victory over worry and anxiety until we begin to treat it as sin. For such it is, it is a deep-seated distrust of the Father, who assures us again and again that even the falling sparrow is in His tender care." ~ Corrie Ten Boom

Jesus said, "What's the use of worrying? What good does it do? Will it add a single day to your life? Of course not! And if worry can't even do such little things as that, what's the use of worrying over bigger things?" (Luke 12:25-26, TLB).

"Do not let your heart be troubled (afraid, cowardly, distressed, agitated). Believe [confidently] in God, adhere to, and rely on and trust in Him, committing to and unto, [have faith, hold on to it, rely on it, keep going and] believe in, adhere to, and trust also in Me," (John 14:1, AMP & AMPC).

The Greek translation for the word "trouble" means to agitate, to cause one inward commotion, take away calmness of mind, to disquiet, make restless, to stir up, to perplex the mind, to strike one's spirit with fear and dread.

Perhaps you're also troubled and can identify with everything listed in those translations. I get it. Oh man, I get it. Life is full of trouble.

Feeling anxious about my to-do list and a potentially difficult conversation I might have with someone, I started worrying about other problems and all the many, many issues in the world. The "what if" scenarios rolled around in my mind, taking away my peace, comfort, and joy.

I felt like a hamster in one of those hamster balls rolling around and not getting anywhere.

A gentle prompting came to stop worrying about the "what ifs" and remember that *whatever* happens, God is in control. His love is unfailing, and He will never leave or forsake His children.

While we lived in the Chicago area, I sat on the top step of our two concrete steps leading to our backyard, wishing we had a deck or patio where our family could sit on cool spring evenings.

When I mentioned that longing to my husband, he advised professional help and/or careful planning before taking on a significant project. Headstrong and a tad impatient, I decided I could build a patio. How hard could it be?

With my hubby safely at work, I skimmed a few project books, made a few notes, ran to the big hardware store, and rented a tiller to prepare the yard. Not just a tiny tiller, I got a BIG one.

Our backdoor neighbor kindly provided the manpower to wrestle the industrial-sized machine out of the van and around to the backyard.

After he left, I started the enormous machine. The engine roared to life. Ah, the power. The blades spun and dug into the ground, sending seismic shocks through the neighborhood.

Unable to control the tiller, I felt like a rodeo rider on a bucking bull as it dragged me halfway across the yard before I finally got my feet planted.

However, once I was immobile, the tiller dug straight down. Down, down, down, it went. It took every ounce of my strength to stop the machine from digging into the Earth's core.

Five miles from China, I finally succeeded in shutting off the out-of-control, overpowering monster.

Collapsing on the ground, I surveyed the potholes, chunks, trenches, and valleys mauling our yard. It was *not* pretty.

My poor hubby returned home and surveyed the damage. Fortunately, he is a very sweet, patient man. After several weeks of hard labor, we created a halfway decent patio.

I learned my lesson (for the moment), and the neighbors still chuckle about the wild, tiller-riding Buffaloe.

Aren't our thoughts often like that out-of-control tiller? Worries drag us all over the place, gouging and mauling our waking and sleeping hours, creating nothing but more problems and anxiety.

Or we plant our feet and dig our thoughts into a bigger hole instead of relying on God in the power of Christ within us.

We don't have to entertain every thought that comes into our heads; we can reject them and take them captive by taking them to Christ. Because as a believer in Christ, we are given the mind of Christ (1 Corinthians 2:16).

Plus, God did not give a spirit of fear but of power, love, and self-control. The Amplified version adds sound judgment and personal discipline [abilities that result in a calm, well-balanced mind, and self-control] (2 Timothy 1:7, AMP).

Take thoughts captive through the power of Christ.

Through Christ's power, we can deny thoughts that waste time, that would cause us to stumble, pull away from God, or deprive us of sleep and soul rest.

When a thought comes to mind, ask yourself the following questions:

- Would this thought be honoring or pleasing to God?

- Will thinking about this thought solve or help anything or anyone?

- Will contemplating this thought bring peace or rest?

- What does God's Word tell me about a thought like this?

Those same questions can be used regarding what we watch, read, and discuss.

Take your thoughts captive by meditating and thinking about whatever is true, honorable, right, pure, lovely, whatever is of good repute, if there is any excellence, anything worthy of praise, and dwell on those things. (Philippians 4:8)

One thing I do when I struggle to control my thoughts is list the attributes or names of God from A to Z.

Praise God who is **A**wesome, **B**eautiful, **C**omforter, **D**eliverer, **E**verlasting, **F**ather, **G**ood, **H**oly, **I**mmutable, **J**oy, **K**ing of kings, **L**ord of lords, **M**erciful, **N**ame above all names, **O**mniscient, **P**owerful, yet **Q**uiets us with His love, **R**ighteous, **S**avior, **T**rue, **U**nfailing, **V**ictorious, **W**onderful, E**X**cellent, **Y**ahweh, God of **Z**ion.

To center your thoughts, think about God's attributes and His names, list them in your mind, and say them out loud.

God is good, kind, patient, all-powerful, almighty, and always in control.

With Christ as our Savior, we are children of the King of kings and Lord of lords. Our Savior has all authority in heaven and earth, and oh, how He loves His children.

Whatever happens, whatever comes, God will be with us through it all. We can trust Him.

> "Worry is belief gone wrong. Because you don't believe that God will get it right. Peace is belief that exhales." ~ Ann Voskamp

Take a deep breath, trust God, and exhale in peace. And let "the peace of Christ [the inner calm of one who walks daily with Him] be the controlling factor in your hearts [deciding and settling questions that arise]. To this peace indeed you were called as members in one body [of believers]. And be thankful [to God always]" (Colossians 3:15, AMP).

Taking back air rights

In urban areas with limited ground space, authorities often grant air rights to use and develop the space above the earth's surface. The concept comes from the Latin phrase, *Cuius est solum, eius est usque ad coelum et ad inferos*, meaning, "Whoever owns the soil, it is theirs up to Heaven and down to Hell."

Have you sold *your* air rights?

What thoughts are you allowing to occupy your mind?

Every moment brings a bombardment of information — news, comments, social media postings, and more—coming at warp speed to fill our minds.

Satan is the prince of the power of the air, the spirit at work in the disobedient [the unbelieving, who fight against the purposes of God] (Ephesians 2:2, AMP).

The devil has an arsenal of devious methods to steal, kill, and destroy to bring fear, division, hate, doubt, and despair. Keeping our minds spinning in the worries of if "this" happens, "that" means "this" will happen. Or if "that" happens, "this" will happen. And all the "this" and "that" will create problems for every "this" and "that" we can imagine.

Remember that for every "this" and every "that," God is always loving, always good, always in control; nothing is impossible for God, and all things work together for the good of those who love Him and are called according to His purpose.

Therefore, when the words "this" or "that" come to mind, insert God into the statement. Put God in whatever scenario, every worry, every concern you have, and rest and trust that God is boundless and timeless.

God is the great I AM. There is no "this" or "that" too big for God to handle. He will be with you and help you through whatever "this" or "that" we face.

The Iron Dome is a 90% effective mobile air defense missile system designed to intercept and destroy short-range projectiles at distances of 2.5 to 90 miles.

As Christians, we're given a 24/7, 100% effective, God-given protective shield of faith with which to extinguish all the flaming arrows of the evil one (Ephesians 6:16).

> "When our minds are on Christ, Satan has little room to maneuver." ~ Billy Graham

With Jesus Christ as our Savior, we are _never_ left defenseless. Christ has **all** authority in heaven and on earth (Matthew 28:18).

His authority reigns in our waking hours and even in the hours we sleep; therefore, we can take every thought captive in His authority.

Christ is with us 24/7. He promises His perfect, calming peace. Whether by night or by day, in every circumstance and every challenge, God will keep in perfect and constant peace the one whose mind is steadfast, committed, and focused on God because they trust and take refuge in God (Isaiah 26:3).

> "One of the best things for your spiritual welfare is to keep recounting the wonders God has done for you, record them in a book, mark the passage in your Bible, and continually refer to it, keep it fresh in your mind." ~ Oswald Chambers

Remember who God is, remember His love, and remember all He has done for you. Remember, "He who is in you is greater than he who is in the world" (1 John 4:4).

God will never forsake you. He will not leave you. He will walk with you through the trials and suffering, and His love will safely carry you close to His heart.

Our Most High God protects and promises never to leave or forsake His children. When thoughts come, focus on Christ, and take thoughts captive in the authority of Christ.

Take back your air rights!

Lisa Buffaloe

Word watch

> "Watch your thoughts, for they become words. Watch your words, for they become actions. Watch your actions, for they become habits. Watch your habits, for they become your character. And watch your character, for it becomes your destiny. What we think, we become." ~ Margaret Thatcher

Your words matter.

My head throbbed with pain from my messed-up neck. The pain radiates with a migraine and feels like someone jabbed a spike in the back of my neck, then extends to my forehead, similar to the sensation of being pulled by a hook placed above my eye.

Tossing and turning during the night, I hoped sleep would relax the muscles. Thankfully, by morning, my neck was feeling much better, and the migraine and hook were gone. Yet when my husband asked how I was, I responded that I was doing a "little" better.

Little? I immediately felt the pain of guilt. I had minimized the truth. I asked the Lord for forgiveness and spoke the truth to my husband — that I was much better.

And then I wondered what if the words I said came true?

What if the words spoken resulted in action?

What if my body heard the word "little" and decided only to have a little healing? Goodness, I sure don't want any little word to result in big consequences.

Our words contain life or death. And every word spoken results in an action internally and externally. Could it be that our words are actually holding us back or causing more problems?

How many times have you heard ...
  I'm doing or feeling a little better.
  We're doing a little better financially.
  The job is a little better.
  The situation is a little better.
  My health is a little better.
  The _____ is a little better.

Perhaps those statements were valid, but what if the words were spoken to minimize the situation, to gain sympathy, or because of doubt, and as a result, we minimized how God is working in our lives?

Have you ever walked around speaking to yourself or others about how tired you are? Or been around someone who complains about everything and everyone?

Spoken words have a positive or negative impact.

The Chladni plate experiment used a tone generator and a metal plate attached to a speaker. Sand was added to the plate, then a tone was played. The sound wave vibrations caused the sand to move and form unpredictable patterns, demonstrating how sound can affect materials.

Dr. Masaru Emoto conducted experiments where he exposed water to positive words, froze it, and then did the same with water exposed to negative words. The ice crystals formed from the positive speech were visually "pleasing," whereas those from the negative speech were "ugly."

The Bible reminds us that death and life are in the power of the tongue, and pleasant words are like a honeycomb, bringing sweetness to the soul and health to the bones. (Proverbs 18:21, Proverbs 16:24).

The words we use, both internally and externally, have an impact.

Kind and pleasant words have a healing effect on both mental and physical health.

Even small words have big consequences.

The enemy is listening. Your soul and body are listening. Speak kindly.

Jesus said that people will have to give an account on the day of judgment for every careless word they have spoken. By our words we will be acquitted, and by our words we will be condemned (Matthew 12:36-37), for there is nothing concealed that will not be disclosed or hidden that will not be made known. What you have said in the dark will be heard in daylight, and what you have whispered in the ear in the inner rooms will be proclaimed from the roofs (Luke 12:2-3).

Words have eternal consequences.

> "Our words can spark a child to accomplish great feats, encourage a husband to conquer the world, fan the dying embers of a friend's broken dreams into flame, encourage a fellow believer to run the race set before her, and draw a lost soul to Christ."
> ~ Sharon Jaynes[27]

Speak the truth. Speak life.

"Let no foul or polluting language, nor evil word nor unwholesome or worthless talk [ever] come out of your mouth, but only such [speech] as is good and beneficial to the spiritual progress of others, as is fitting to the need and the occasion, that it may be a blessing and give grace (God's favor) to those who hear it," (Ephesians 4:29, AMPC).

Use your words for God's kingdom, to honor and glorify Him. Make your words gracious, seasoned with salt, so that you may know how to answer each person (Colossians 4:6).

Heavenly Father, to live in Your freedom, "Let the words of my mouth and the meditation of my heart be acceptable in Your sight, O Lord, my strength and my Redeemer," (Psalm 19:14, NKJV).

The calm center

Jesus said, Love the Lord your God with all your heart, with all your soul, and with all your mind (Matthew 22:37).

Loving God is an invitation with a beautiful circular truth.

By directing our love towards God, we become better able to experience His love. The greater our love for God, the greater our love becomes for God and others. When we focus on God's attributes—His love, power, strength, goodness, and comfort—our awareness of them grows, shifting our focus away from worldly issues and troubles.

> "The one thing that keeps us from the possibility of worrying is bringing God in as the greatest factor in all our calculations. If we are obsessed by God, nothing else can get into our lives—not concerns, nor tribulations, nor worries. And now we understand why our Lord so emphasized the sin of worrying. How can we dare to be so absolutely unbelieving when God totally surrounds us? To be obsessed by God is to have an effective barricade against all the assaults of the enemy." ~ Oswald Chambers[28]

Oh, to be obsessed with God, infatuated with God, and delighting in God. Psalm 37:4 invites you to delight yourself in the Lord, and He will give you the desires of your heart.

The more we delight in God, the more we long to please Him and desire the things He desires.

> "A person is known by the passion that drives him day after day through thick and thin. What is needed today is passion, but more defined, a deep desire to know God as He desires to be known. I desire to know God in all the beauty of the divine unfolding."
> ~ A. W. Tozer[29]

Oh, may God be our passion.

Loving the Lord with all our heart, soul, mind, and strength, and loving our neighbor as ourselves, means we are living and focused on God's love. The middle stays connected to the unmoving.

> "Let us occupy ourselves entirely in knowing God. The more we know Him, the more we will desire to know Him. As love increases with knowledge, the more we know God, the more we will truly love Him. We will learn to love Him equally in times of distress or in times of great joy." ~ Brother Lawrence

By concentrating on our steadfast and ever-loving God, the world's problems will be cast aside, much like a pinwheel shedding water as it spins.

Tropical cyclones or hurricanes are often massive, yet they contain a calm spot at their core called the eye of the storm. In the same way, Jesus offers a blessed invitation for unmoving, solid, eternal peace and hope.

> "In every time of storm and stress, the presence of Jesus and the love which flows from the Cross bring peace and serenity and calm." ~ William Barclay

Jesus said not to fret or worry because God cares for you. Instead of worrying, pray about everything. Tell God what you need and thank him for all he has done. Let petitions and praises shape your worries into prayers, letting God know your concerns. Before you know it, a sense of God's wholeness, everything coming together for good, will come and settle you down. It's wonderful what happens when Christ displaces worry at the center of your life (1 Peter 5:7, Philippians 4:6, MSG).

Though we will encounter problems, the peace of Christ remains constant.

In <u>Me</u>, Jesus invites, "You may have [perfect] peace and confidence. In the world, you have tribulation and trials and distress and frustration, but be of good cheer [take courage; be confident, certain, undaunted!] For I have overcome the world. [I have deprived it of power to harm you and have conquered it for you.]" (John 16:33, AMPC).

"For the hearts that will cease focusing on themselves, there is 'the peace of God, which transcends all understanding' (Phil 4:7); 'quietness and trust' (Isa.30:15), which is the source of all strength; a 'great peace' that will never 'make them stumble' (Ps. 119:165); and a deep rest which the world can never give nor take away. Deep within the center of the soul is a chamber of peace where God lives and where, if we will enter it and quiet all the other sounds, we can hear His 'gentle whisper' (1 Kings 19:12). And even in the busiest life, there is a place where we may dwell alone with God in eternal stillness." ~ L. B. Cowman[30]

The challenging adventure

> "In this life, we'll never have all the answers on the first page of a new journey. Nor will God allow us to read the last page of a story we're not willing to step into. But we do have a choice. Will we pursue this season of life, with all the unknowns, with or without the Father? Our decision reveals whether we hunger more for guarantees ... or God." ~ Allen Arnold[31]

The line "Your mission, should you choose to accept it" from the "Mission: Impossible" TV show and movie franchise gives agents the option to accept a task.

If at birth I had been told what awaited in my future, I would **not** have accepted my mission. I was molested by a babysitter, assaulted by two guys, raped, divorced, stalked, had cancer, faced the death of loved ones, fought years of chronic illness, and had multiple surgeries and medical procedures. And that's only a small part of the journey.

Some aspects of my life have been positive, while others have been quite negative. Yet every experience, heartache, and difficulty has blessed me with a framework to share God's amazing grace and His spiritual, physical, and emotional healing and restoration.

God never wastes our time or pain.

Jesus never said following Him would be easy. He knew we would face trouble, be persecuted and suffer, and that difficult times would be part of our journey, yet Jesus reminded us He has overcome the world.

> "Christians do not go through tribulations to get to heaven, but Christians go through tribulations because they are going to heaven." ~ Jack Andrews

We can trust that the One who conquered the world will help us conquer everything we face in this world.

> "God will give us the strength and resources we need to live through any situation in life that He ordains." ~ Billy Graham

During a difficult time in my life, I slept with a loaded pistol under my pillow. I needed protection.

I also needed strength, so I joined a gym and lifted weights.

My gym buddies would watch over me, offering support and assisting if my muscles gave out while I was lifting heavy weights. My friends encouraged me to continue with the repetitions and to lift more weight than I thought possible.

I didn't look like a bodybuilder, but my body became lean and strong. With each increase in weight and resistance, my strength and confidence levels rose.

From the pain comes gain.

> "God does not give us overcoming life: He gives us life as we overcome. The strain is the strength. If there is no strain, there is no strength." ~ Oswald Chambers

Beyond suffering come great blessings.

Paul wrote to rejoice in our sufferings, knowing that suffering produces endurance (Romans 5:3)

> "Never run from suffering, but bear it silently, patiently, and submissively with the assurance that it is God's way of instilling iron into your spiritual life ... Your time is not wasted, for God is simply putting you through His iron regimen. Your iron crown of suffering precedes your golden crown of glory. And iron is entering your soul to make it strong and brave." ~ F. B. Meyer

One day, while polishing our wooden coffee table, I noticed the wood's knots, rings, and scars—shaped by growth and surroundings, its challenges and tests—gave it character and beauty.

Scars tell of the journey.

I have many scars on my body. Some came from funny stories, some did not, yet they all changed me.

Life leaves scars. Internal and external marks of what we have been through. But those scars are precious. They are proof of survival during the fires of life. They are rich, deep, and strengthening. They glow with the testimony of God's faithfulness. Because no matter how deep the scars, God's love runs deeper, and His love turns everything into beauty.

> "The irons of sorrow and loss, the burdens carried as a youth, and the soul's struggle against sin all contribute to developing an iron tenacity and strength of purpose, as well as endurance and fortitude. And these traits make up the indispensable foundation and framework of noble character. The world is looking for iron leaders, iron armies, iron tendons, and muscles of steel. But God is looking for iron saints, and since there is no way to impart iron into His people's moral nature except by letting them suffer, He allows them to suffer. Your time is not wasted, for God is simply putting you through His iron regimen. Your iron crown of suffering precedes your golden crown of glory, and iron is entering your soul to make it strong and brave." ~ F. B. Meyer

Will we be iron saints?

> "There are many blessings we will never obtain if we are unwilling to accept and endure suffering. There are certain joys that can come to us only through sorrow. There are revelations of God's divine truth that we will receive only when the lights of earth have been extinguished. And there are harvests that will grow only once the plow has done its work." ~ Lettie Cowman[32]

Even though life's hardships often appear meaningless, agonizing, and upsetting, God's marvelous work unfolds through and beyond suffering.

Glorious endings come for those who have been refined by fire and tested in the sorrows of life.

> "Her past was a tragedy to lament. But her future was an epic to anticipate." ~ Mark Buchanan[33]

I love that line!

What if we realized that truth?

With Christ in our lives, no matter what we have gone through or may experience in the future, an epic ending awaits!

> "Only through experiences of trial and suffering can the soul be strengthened, ambition inspired, and success achieved."
> ~ Helen Keller

"In this you greatly rejoice, though now for a little while, if need be, you have been grieved by various trials, that the genuineness of your faith, being much more precious than gold that perishes, though it is tested by fire, may be found to praise, honor, and glory at the revelation of Jesus Christ," (1 Peter 1:6-7, NKJV).

Consider it all joy when you encounter various trials, James wrote, knowing that the testing of your faith produces endurance. And let endurance have its perfect result, so that you may be perfect and complete, lacking in nothing. Not only that, but rejoice in your sufferings, knowing that suffering produces endurance, and endurance produces character, and character produces hope, and hope does not put us to shame, because God's love has been poured into your hearts through the Holy Spirit who has been given to us, (James 1:2-4, Romans 5:3-6).

> "Trials are divine sculptors; they chisel away at our pride, carving us into humble vessels of God's grace." ~ John Knox

What if we looked at our trials as opportunities?

> "We are faced with a series of great opportunities brilliantly disguised as impossible situations." ~ Chuck Swindoll

Nothing is impossible for God.

> "The Red Sea may roll before us; the desert may entrap us; the enemy may press on our heels. The past may seem implausible and the future impossible, but God works in ways we cannot see. He will make a way of escape for His weary, but waiting, children. So, take a deep breath and recall this deeper secret of the Christian life: when you are in a difficult place, realize that the Lord either placed you there or allowed you to be there, for reasons perhaps known for now only to Himself. The same God who led you in will lead you out." ~ Robert Morgan[34]

Difficulties are an invitation to grow closer to the Lord and discover truths hidden in the darkness of suffering. Trials and suffering grow faith, perfecting, producing endurance, character, and hope.

Apart from the very nasty things that happened when I was younger, I've struggled for years with health issues.

One day, I posted a smiling photo of myself to update one of my social media profiles. The outward picture did not show what was happening inside.

X-rays and an MRI show my neck is a mess with some areas collapsed, one disc sticking out one way, another the other way, nerves are pinched and squashed, and so arthritic the discs are fusing. The entire neck now curves in the wrong direction. When my neck hurts, it often triggers headaches and migraines. The surgeon grimly informed me that a four-level surgery offered no guarantee of pain relief.

Since then, I've had numerous pain injections, Medical Branch blocks, and an ablation to destroy the neck nerves. The last procedure blessed me with several weeks of wonderful total relief. Praise the Lord! I give thanks for an elevated desk to use while I write, which keeps my posture straight and relieves neck strain. Thank God, I do have some days when I don't need pain medication.

Nothing happening inside my body is visible to others.

Besides the neck problems, X-rays and an MRI show bulging discs in my lower back, squashing the nerves. I have stage three kidney disease and a cyst on one kidney. A bone-deep hip pain started and didn't go away. X-rays and MRI showed a soft tissue tumor sitting next to major arteries, nerves, and other organs. The surgery to remove the softball-sized tumor went well, and thankfully, the tumor was benign. The presence of a tear and arthritis in the hip indicates that a hip replacement will be needed.

If one part of my body doesn't hurt, another part hurts. It seems there is a competition to see which area can garner the most attention.

Whine, whine, whine, and whimper. Sorry about that.

Life is painful, isn't it?

Compared with others' struggles, my problems are very insignificant. Your list of issues may make mine look like a walk in the park on a beautiful day.

All of us face adversity.

You have your own hidden pain and sorrow. I'm so sorry. Life is hard, difficult, and, at times, agonizing.

> "Nothing that is not part of God's will is allowed to come into the life of someone who trusts and obeys Him. This truth should be enough to make our life one of ceaseless thanksgiving and joy, because God's will is the most hopeful, pleasant, and glorious thing in the world. It is the continuous working of His omnipotent power for our benefit, with nothing to prevent it, if we remain surrendered and believing. We live fascinating lives if we are living in the center of God's will. All the attacks that Satan hurls at us through the sins of others are not only powerless to harm us, but are transformed into blessings along the way."
> ~ Hannah Whitall Smith

The most difficult times can often lead to the best of times.

In God's economy, gain can come from loss, because God works all things to work together for good to those who love God, to those who are called according to His purpose (Romans 8:28).

We might not see the good, but good will come.

> "We often pray to be delivered from afflictions, and even trust God that we will be. But we do not pray for Him to make us what we should be while in the midst of the afflictions. Nor do we pray that we would be able to live within them, for however long they may last, in the complete awareness that we are held and sheltered by the Lord and can therefore continue within them without suffering any harm." ~ L. B. Cowman[35]

The road through this life, on the way to heaven, is never easy.

> "God has had one Son without sin, but he has never had one child without suffering." ~ Charles Spurgeon

Many deal with things no one knows about—unseen physical and mental pain, grief, pain from past problems, pain from today's issues, and prayers yet to be answered.

> "The deepest things I have learned in my own life have come from the deepest suffering. And out of the deepest waters and the hottest fires have come the deepest things I know about God."
> ~ Elisabeth Elliot

Sometimes, life just hurts.

Some days, all one can do is curl up in God's arms and weep.

A little girl was late getting back from school, and her mother scolded her, demanding an explanation for her delay.

The girl replied that she had been helping another girl in trouble. Curious, the mom asked what her daughter had done.

The little girl answered, "I sat down and helped her cry."

There is a time to weep and a time to mourn. And we are to weep with those who weep. (Ecclesiastes 3:4, Romans 12:15).

> "Our vision is so limited we can hardly imagine a love that does not show itself in protection from suffering. The love of God did not protect His own Son. He will not necessarily protect us — not from anything it takes to make us like His Son. A lot of hammering and chiseling and purifying by fire will have to go into the process." ~ Elisabeth Elliot

Whatever you have gone through, whatever you are going through, or whatever you might go through in the future, Jesus knows how you feel. Christ was perfect and sinless and went around doing good, healing thousands, feeding multitudes, and preaching the good news. Yet, Jesus was hated, persecuted, falsely accused, beaten, and crucified.

Jesus understands suffering; He will be with you and never leave or forsake you. God understands suffering. The Lord comforts His people and will have compassion on His afflicted ones (Isaiah 49:13).

God is the "Father of our Lord Jesus Christ, the Father of sympathy (pity and mercy) and the God [Who is the Source] of every comfort (consolation and encouragement), Who comforts (consoles and encourages) us in every trouble (calamity and affliction), so that we may also be able to comfort (console and encourage) those who are in any kind of trouble or distress, with the comfort (consolation and encouragement) with which we ourselves are comforted (consoled and encouraged) by God," (2 Corinthians 1:3-4, AMPC).

Everyone is subject to pain, whether it originates in the body or the mind.

How often have we wondered how God could love us when He allows suffering?

The enemy whispers or screams —

If God loved you, you wouldn't suffer.

If God loved you, your loved one wouldn't have left or died.

If God loved you, you wouldn't have been through what you've been through.

If God were loving, you wouldn't be in pain, you wouldn't be sick, you wouldn't have trouble, your job would be good, your kids would love you, you'd have plenty of money, on and on and on.

The truth is — <u>God is always good and always loving.</u>

God is love, and He is loving whether or not we hurt. God's love is not changed by our pain or the world's pain.

We live in a fallen world, and suffering will exist until we are home in heaven with perfect bodies.

> "Afflictions are often the dark settings God uses to mount the jewels of His children's gifts, causing them to shine even brighter. God trains His soldiers not in tents of ease and luxury but by causing them to endure lengthy marches and difficult service. He makes them wade across streams, swim through rivers, climb mountains, and walk many tiring miles with heavy backpacks." ~ Charles H. Spurgeon

Jesus told us not to worry about tomorrow, that He will never leave or forsake us.

> "Will you keep going when you don't know why? When you can't get any answers that would make the pain go away, will you still say, 'My Lord,' even though his ways are not clear to you? Will you keep going—with all the grace and grit and faith you can muster—and live in hope that one day God will set everything right. Will you trust that God is good? Ultimately, the choice everyone faces is the choice between hope and despair.
> Jesus says, 'Choose hope.'" ~ John Ortberg[36]

Count it all joy, James wrote.
Rejoice always and pray without ceasing, advised Paul.
Peter said to cast all our anxiety on God.
That advice isn't easy. Yet what they shared has power.
Praying, casting our cares on the Lord, rejoicing, trusting and relying on God, and turning to the Lord shifts our focus away from our difficulties and suffering, where we find God's presence, joy, and peace.
Casting is to throw upon, place upon, and give our cares to God. Cast your burden on the Lord [releasing the weight of it], and He will sustain you. Casting all your cares, all anxieties, all worries, and all concerns, once and for all on Him, for He cares about you [with deepest affection, and watches over you very carefully] (Psalm

55:22, 1 Peter 5:7, AMPC).

Casting recreates. The book of Exodus recounts the building of the tabernacle, where a worker cast metal into a fire, creating something beautiful and new.

Casting brings peace. As we cast our worries and concerns on God, He restores what the enemy meant for evil. God makes all things beautiful in His time and works all things for good for those who love Him.

Casting our cares on God is a gift. God cares for you; you can trust His unfailing love. Cast your burdens on the Lord, and the weight will roll off your shoulders and onto God's strong, loving, all-powerful shoulders. Fear will be cast out, and your mind and soul can rest in His peace.

Therefore, cast the weight of your burdens on the Lord's mighty, affectionate, all-powerful shoulders.

Keep going; God's got you in His strong, faithful, comforting arms.

Brave suffering

During pain and suffering, what if we prayed not only for God's healing, comfort, and rescue but also for the ability to trust God and be brave?

> "We must try to make our sick friend braver to endure his sufferings." ~ J. R. Miller

What if we were brave during our suffering?

> "Great character is made not through luxurious living but through suffering. And the world does not forget people of great character." ~ Cortland Myers

Although a conscientious objector, Desmond Doss served as a combat medic during World War II. Since Doss refused to carry a gun, his fellow soldiers and commanding officer made his life miserable.

During the spring of 1948 in Okinawa, Doss's unit was ordered to ascend a steep, rocky cliff known as Hacksaw Ridge. On the plateau, the soldiers were met by thousands of heavily armed Japanese soldiers. In one of the Pacific's most brutal conflicts, the fighting was intense, with soldiers describing it as a hailstorm of bullets from enemy weapons.

The wounded had no way of escaping. With gunfire and explosions erupting, Doss crawled across the ground, tending to the injured soldiers. He moved the badly hurt men to the cliff's edge, used a rope to secure them, and then carefully lowered them to the medical team positioned below.

While in Okinawa, Doss was wounded four times. Despite Desmond's injuries, even though he was under horrible enemy fire, he continued going and is credited with saving seventy-five wounded soldiers. He said he had been praying the whole time. Praying that the Lord would help him get one more. One veteran reported it was as if God had his hand on Desmond's shoulder.

Even though Desmond suffered ridicule and abuse from others, he continued serving. Despite the gunfire all around him, despite his own injuries, Desmond kept on saving injured soldiers.

In our suffering, will we reach out to help others?

> "God doesn't promise to always save you *externally*, but he always promises to save you *internally*—to give you faith for fear, peace in your problems, security in the storm, and faith enough to finish. He will never leave you nor forsake you, no matter how difficult the task. He who has appointed and anointed will assist you with the power to finish." ~ Jill Briscoe[37]

John Harper was traveling aboard the Titanic. When the ship struck the iceberg, John yelled for the women, children, and unsaved to get into the lifeboats. As the boat sank, John, along with other people, went into the icy waters. He was seen frantically swimming from person to person, trying to lead them to Christ.

At a survivor's meeting, a man shared that John had given him his life vest and led him to Christ. He said Mr. Harper swam from person to person, but because of the intense cold, had grown too weak to swim.

Mr. Harper's last words before going under in the frigid waters were, "Believe on the Name of the Lord Jesus and you will be saved."

Despite John's own suffering, he used his words, his very last breath, to tell others about Christ and His saving grace.

Will we be brave in our suffering?

> "It is from suffering that the strongest souls ever known have emerged; the world's greatest display of character is seen in those who exhibit the scars of sorrow; the martyrs of the ages have worn their coronation robes that have glistened with fire, yet through their tears and sorrow have seen the gates of heaven." ~ Chapin

Many revival movements throughout history were birthed in prayer from those who could not leave their beds and had little physical strength.

In 1872, Marianne Adlard, a bedridden woman, prayed fervently for a spiritual awakening in her church. Her prayers were the match that led to a major revival led by Dwight L. Moody in England.

Because of prayer, revivals were born, individuals were saved, and comfort and encouragement were given.

Will we use our time of suffering to pray for others?

No matter how weak your body, no matter how deep your suffering, the prayer of a righteous person has great power (James 5:16).

Helen Roseveare, a medical doctor/missionary in Africa, had prayed for years for reconciliation and unity between European missionaries and their African colleagues. In October 1964, after the start of a horrific civil war, she was beaten and brutalized by guerrilla soldiers.

After that savage night, she was taken with other Europeans to stand before a firing squad. Arguments broke out among the rebel factions, and the group was returned to house arrest. A few days later, the Europeans were taken out, lined up, and again arguments broke out — this time because of Helen's bruised and battered face.

She was asked by the commander who had hurt her. Helen answered that he was one of his subordinates. The commander struck her and called her a liar. Helen responded that she wasn't lying and could name the man. Furious, the commander said he would call a "people's court."

That same night, they threw her into the back of a pickup truck. As dawn broke, they entered a village where the rebels had rounded up men to be part of the people's court.

Scared, alone, hardly able to see out of her badly swollen eyes, Helen tried to answer the rapid-fire questions from the rebels. Then came the moment when the crowd was told to condemn her as a liar.

Helen wrote, "I became conscious of a strange and growing sound—a sound I'd never heard before and probably will never hear again. Several hundred strong farming men broke down and wept. Men crying. Suddenly, instead of seeing me as the hated white foreigner, they saw me as 'their doctor,' one they had learned to love and respect through the past twelve years of service. They swept forward, driving the rebel soldiers out of the way, and took me in their arms and hugged me. 'She's ours. She's ours,' they kept repeating. God had answered four years of prayer in that moment! I had no idea that He might ask me to be part of the process involved in bringing about that restored unity. It was as though God whispered to me, 'Can you accept the suffering now? My purpose is to restore the unity between the national and foreign communities, something for which you have prayed so fervently.'"[38]

Weeks later, 200 people were attacked by rebel soldiers and herded into two single-family homes. One of the women expecting a baby was in great pain. Helen, being the only available doctor, was commanded by two armed soldiers to check on the woman.

Arriving at the packed house, Helen noted she knew almost everyone there. She had been their doctor for years, caring for their sick, bringing their babies into the world, and operating as needed. Yet, overwhelmed by their situation, none of them looked at her or gave any sign of recognition.

Helen prayed, asking God why she was really there. Then clarity came. The soldiers spoke Lingala, knew a smattering of Swahili, and a few words in French, but no Greek or English.

While examining the woman, Helen carried on a conversation in five languages.

She wrote, "phrase by phrase, three languages dealing with a medical examination and later with prescribed treatment, and two languages telling them as simply as I could, in the limited time available, of the Saviour's death on Calvary in their place that they might know the forgiveness of sins."[39]

Then, without closing her eyes, she led the captives in a prayer of confession of sin, asking for forgiveness, and that their hearts would be open to receive Christ's salvation. As she left the home, still escorted by the soldiers, everyone looked up, eyes full of new hope, grasping her hands and thanking her for coming. And she knew without a doubt that some had responded to God's grace.

Back at her home that night, she prayed, asking why the people had not responded to her preaching of the gospel for the last twelve years. The Lord reminded her, "They know what you suffered that Thursday night six weeks ago. And were not some of them also there at the people's court that Tuesday night? Didn't they see your bruised and swollen eyes, your cut and bloody face? If you hadn't suffered that night in late October, they would have been tempted to say in their hearts, 'What does she know about it?' But because they know that you suffered then, despite all that they have suffered now in these last twenty-four hours, I have been able to open their hearts to respond to My love and to listen to your words."[40]

Helen's suffering — her scars, her wounds — opened doors and opened hearts to Christ's love. God turned what the enemy meant for evil into good.

When suffering comes, when life beats bloody, we can trust that God has a purpose beyond our imagination. There is so much more happening than we can see and understand.

God never wastes our time or pain. There are blessings beyond the battle scars.

God's heart, God's unfailing love, is for people to know His Son, Jesus Christ, so that they will be saved. God, in His kindness and tender mercies, will at times put us in difficult situations to help us grow and to help others, for God desires all people to be saved and come to the knowledge of the truth (1 Timothy 2:4).

> "If God eliminated the problem, He would have eliminated the particular kind of blessing which it bears." Elisabeth Elliott

People need to know about Christ; they need to know those who have gone through hardships and can identify with their suffering. They need to know the Savior. And your story, your scars, can point to the wounds of Christ who suffered, died, and rose again, proving His love for all.

"We are persecuted by others, but God has not forsaken us. We may be knocked down, but not out. We continually share in the death of Jesus in our own bodies so that the resurrection life of Jesus will be revealed through our humanity. We consider living to mean that we are constantly being handed over to death for Jesus' sake so that the life of Jesus will be revealed through our humanity" (2 Corinthians 4:9-11, TPT).

"After you have suffered a little while, the God of all grace [Who imparts all blessing and favor], Who has called you to His [own] eternal glory in Christ Jesus, will Himself complete and make you what you ought to be, establish and ground you securely, and strengthen, and settle you," (1 Peter 5:10, AMPC).

Beyond the wound

We've all been wounded. The devil wants people to stay trapped in the offenses done against them.

If we keep our hurts from God and decline His healing, our damaged areas will skew our views of the world, others, and ourselves.

Fortunately, God is our Great Physician, Jehovah-Rapha, the God who heals. Jesus came to bind the broken-hearted, heal wounds, and heal lives. He restores sight to the blind and sets captives free. Nothing is impossible for God, and nothing can stop the love of God.

> "Our dear Lord cares for the broken pieces of our lives, the fragments of all we meant to do, the little that we have to gather up and offer, and He will use even these fragments. He will not let even the least of our little broken things to be lost." ~ Amy Carmichael[41]

As Christians, we don't have to walk as the wounded. Jesus offers freedom, rest, and healing for every wound and every soul that comes to Him.

The compassion, grace, and mercy of Jesus Christ restore sight to those blinded by sins committed against us and sins we have committed. Jesus restores what the enemy meant for evil and makes all things new. For "we know [with great confidence] that God [who is deeply concerned about us] causes all things to work together [as a plan] for good for those who love God, to those who are called according to His plan and purpose," (Romans 8:28, AMP).

Please don't let the devil keep you trapped in your wound. Come to the One wounded for you, who reaches out with nail-scarred hands to bring healing and restoration.

> "When we press past the pain in prayer, when we press into Jesus, peace sutures bleeding hearts and holds them tenderly until they heal." ~ Gwen Smith[42]

God is the merciful God of all comfort who heals the brokenhearted and binds up their wounds [healing their pain and comforting their sorrow] (2 Corinthians 1:3, Psalm 147:3, AMP).

> "I have prayed, and still pray, that if you are called to participate in the sufferings of Jesus Christ, you may partake also of his patience and submission. You will find the Lord at all times near your heart when you seek him by a simple and sincere desire to do and suffer his will. He will be your support and consolation in this time of trouble, if you go to him, not with fear and agitation of spirit, but with calm, confiding love." ~ Madam Guyon

Even when I wallowed in the mud of sin or self-pity, God picked me up, dusted me off, and set me on my feet again, granting His unfailing, unmerited grace.

God has never failed to bless me with food when the pantry was bare, nor to supply my every need.

> "God has never failed me. Even in my greatest difficulties, heaviest trials, and deepest poverty and need. He has never failed me. Because I was enabled by God's grace to trust Him. He has always come to my aid. I delight in speaking well of His name."
> ~ George Mueller

And every day God never fails to lavish His extravagant love and grant beauty through His marvelous creation.

God has never failed to heal the wounds of the past, and never failed to hold me close in times of sorrow.

Even on days when I wondered where He was and why my situation didn't change, God has never failed me. Even when I couldn't see what would happen next (even when I didn't like what would happen next), God has never failed me.

And He will never fail you.

Glory beyond the pain

Jesus loved his friends Martha, Mary, and Lazarus (John 11), yet when He heard Lazarus was sick, He waited two more days before traveling to see them.

Jesus waited until Lazarus was dead.

> "Jesus refrained from going not because He did not love them but because He did love them." ~ L. B. Cowman

Jesus waited to show the glory of God's power in raising him from the dead. Jesus said, "Did I not say to you that if you would believe you would see the glory of God?" (John 11:40, NKJV).

Glory lies beyond pain. Sometimes, God's vast and flawless love allows us to experience pain so that we can see His glory in a way we couldn't before.

> "Who can estimate the great debt we owe to suffering and pain? If not for them, we would have little capacity for many of the great virtues of the Christian life. Where would our faith be if not for the trials that test it, or patience, without anything to endure or experience without tribulations to develop it?" ~ L. B. Cowman

God promises, "I will give you the treasures of darkness and hidden wealth of secret places, so that you may know that it is I, the Lord, the God of Israel, who calls you by your name," (Isaiah 45:3, NASB).

> "God has gone before us and buried a treasure in every problem and stored rich truths in every minute of darkness we will face. The only way we can discover that treasure is to embrace the problem as an opportunity to trust God and uncover a new seed of victory." ~ Mary Southerland

During times of difficulty, I'd prefer to get out of that difficulty as soon as possible. However, the process through hardships is where growth is found.

> "Trials are not 'chastisement'. No earthly father goes on chastising a loving child. That is a common thought about suffering, but I am quite sure it is a wrong thought. Paul's suffering were not that, nor are yours. They are battle wounds. They are signs of high confidence—honours. The Father holds His children very close to His heart when they are going through such rough places as this." ~ Amy Carmichael[43]

Trials lead to treasure not found on an easy road.
Trials prove genuine faith.
Trials bring endurance, character, and hope.
Trials polish the soul.
Trials bless with the crown of life.

Blessed is the man who remains steadfast under trial, for when he has stood the test he will receive the crown of life, which God has promised to those who love him" (James 1:12, ESV).

> "In heaven we shall see that we had not one trial too many."
> ~ Charles Spurgeon

Cutting off spent flowers, or dead-heading, redirects the plant's energy away from seed development and toward the creation of new blossoms.

Sometimes, when we're put in difficult situations, it feels like a part of us is cut off. Yet, with God's gentle touch, fresh growth will come.

> "If I would serve Christ and my fellow men, as He served me, I must be willing—indeed, I must expect—to be broken to release the 'fragrance of the knowledge of Him' (2 Cor. 2:14). We do not need to fear the breaking, because we are held in His nail-pierced hands, but He cannot feed others through us if we resist the breaking." ~ Helen Roseveare[44]

Gideon and his army broke their clay jars to bring forth light. Mary broke her alabaster jar, releasing a beautiful fragrance for her Savior. A little boy donated his loaves and fishes, which Jesus broke to feed a multitude.

The broken body of our Savior, Jesus Christ, was broken to give new life and eternal hope.

> "God knows that you can withstand your trial, or else He would not have given it to you. His trust in you explains the trials of your life, no matter how severe they may be. God knows your strength, and He measures it to the last inch. Remember, no trial has ever been given to anyone that was greater than that person's strength, through God, to endure it." ~ L. B. Cowman[45]

For our momentary affliction is preparing for us an eternal weight of glory beyond all comparison.

> "We move in time, but God operates in eternity." ~ David Jeremiah

When going through difficulties, let's ask for spiritual eyes to see what God is showing us, what we can learn, what God is doing and revealing about Himself to us and others, and how God can use us for His Kingdom.

The journey is only part of the process.

Missionary Jack Scholes told the story of a carpenter building a cupboard. The man cut and prepared each board, drilling holes for the nails, then hammered each one into place and covered them with wood filler. When he completed the project, not a single nail was visible.

> Jack asked, are we "willing to be nails in the hands of the Master Carpenter? Would we grumble at the painful blows of the hammer, or would we remember that the hammer was held by the nail-pierced hands? Remember, the Lord has only one purpose ultimately for each one of us — to make us more like Jesus. He is interested in your relationship with Himself. Let Him take you and mould you as He will; all the rest will take its rightful place."
> ~ Jack Scholes"[46]

Everything you've gone through, with God's help, can strengthen your faith, trust, and confidence in Him. Moreover, your experiences can be used to help those who are going through or will experience similar hardships.

> "Nothing but the great trials and dangers we have experienced would ever have led some of us to know Him as we do, to trust Him as we have, and to draw from Him the great measure of His grace so indispensable during our times of greatest need. Difficulties and obstacles are God's challenges to our faith. When we are confronted with hindrances that block our path of service, we are to recognize them as vessels for faith and then to fill them with the fullness and complete sufficiency of Jesus."
> ~ A. B. Simpson[47]

Through Christ, we "have access by faith into this [remarkable state of] grace in which we [firmly and safely and securely] stand. Let us rejoice in our hope and the confident assurance of [experiencing and enjoying] the glory of [our great] God [the manifestation of His excellence and power]. And not only this, but [with joy] let us exult in our sufferings and rejoice in our hardships, knowing that hardship (distress, pressure, trouble) produces patient endurance; and endurance, proven character (spiritual maturity); and proven character, hope and confident assurance [of eternal salvation]" (Romans 5:2-4, AMP).

> "Our trials are great opportunities, but all too often we simply see them as large obstacles. If only we would recognize every difficult situation as something God has chosen to prove His love to us, each obstacle would then become a place of shelter and rest, and a demonstration to others of His inexpressible power. If we would look for the signs of His glorious handiwork, then every cloud would indeed become a rainbow, and every difficult mountain path would become one of ascension, transformation, and glorification. If we would look at our past, most of us would realize that the times we endured the greatest stress and felt that every path was blocked were the very times our heavenly Father chose to do the kindest things for us and bestow His richest blessings. God's most beautiful jewels are often delivered in rough packages by very difficult people, but within the package we will find the very treasures of the King's palace and the Bridegroom's love." ~ A. B. Simpson

When suffering continues

> "There is more to life than being healthy, than being happy, than being problem-free, than being comfortable, than feeling good, than getting what we want, than being healed. There is more to life even than *living*! And the 'more to life' is the development of our faith to the extent that our very lives display His glory!"
> ~ Anne Graham Lotz[48]

God can heal in an instant, yet illness sometimes persists.

During the six years I was plagued by undiagnosed Lyme Disease, doctors searched for a reason my body seemed in self-destruct mode. Scans, blood tests, nerve tests, any kind of test, I probably had it done as I suffered from tumors, cysts, numbness, headaches, migraines, horrible dizziness, a swollen jugular vein, kidney infections, kidney stones, eye problems, nerve damage, hearing loss, and bleeding issues in areas that should <u>not</u> bleed.

The first round of diagnoses included labyrinthitis, Ménière's disease, rheumatoid arthritis, Lupus, multiple sclerosis, autoimmune inner ear disease, and many other very unpleasant conditions.

There were days my dizziness was so intense that I had to stay as still as possible. The crystal-like structures sitting on the tiny hairs in the inner ear that sense movement were firing at random times, making my body think I was riding one of those horrid teacup rides at a county fair.

Reading, even watching television, was out of the question, and all I could do was lie in bed or in the recliner and try not to move.

My only options were to rest, wait, and pray.

> "There is no music during a musical rest, but the rest is part of the making of the music. God does not write the music of our lives without a plan. Our part is to learn the tune and not be discouraged during the rests." ~ John Ruskin

After Lyme Disease was finally diagnosed, the battle continued for another six years. Every antibiotic known to man (both orally and intravenously) was administered to rid the bacteria attacking my body.

Yet in the dark, desperate times, when life stopped, God met me.

> "In my deepest wound, I saw Your glory, and it dazzled me."
> ~ St. Augustine

Family, friends, and I offered desperate prayers for healing, yet even with medical help, the disease continued to ravage my body.

Praise the Lord that even during my long Lyme battle, God blessed me with some good days, and I could go about my life as though nothing was wrong.

Some people said that if I had enough faith, recited the proper prayers, used the product they were selling, quoted certain Bible verses, or had enough positive vibes, I would be healed. That was not helpful and only added to the pain.

Job was considered a righteous man by God, and yet he suffered in horrible ways.

Paul advised Timothy to take care of his stomach and frequent ailments (1 Timothy 5:23). Paul didn't lecture Timothy, tell him that if he had enough faith, he wouldn't be sick, or quote prayers. Paul simply gave comforting advice.

We are told to comfort others with the comfort we are given by our merciful God (2 Corinthians 1:3-5).

If we never suffered, how would we know how to give comfort?

The great preacher, Charles Spurgeon, suffered bouts of depression and anxiety. Because of his debilitating physical and psychological conditions, he was often bedridden for weeks. Yet, Spurgeon said his suffering enabled him to encourage and comfort many hurting people. In his fifty-seven years, he authored over 135 books and published more than 3,500 sermons.

No matter how mighty our faith, illness and suffering will hit every single one of us.

Do I believe God can heal? Absolutely! I have **no** doubt. I've received God's divine healing on multiple occasions. And God even healed my Lyme Disease!

God can change anything — any situation or circumstance — yet hardships will still arise.

> "Eternal glory is not a reward reserved for stoic endurance. It is the conviction that God is weaving purpose into the threads of our suffering—often in ways invisible from where we stand. The work of heaven's workshop is slow and patient: mending, re-weaving, shaping. Sometimes the design doesn't show for years. Sometimes the evidence arrives as a hymn on the radio, as a friend's hand at just the right time, as a Scripture verse landing differently than it did before. When suffering feels unrelenting, two small gospel habits have helped me re-see: Name it plainly. Don't dress sorrow in tidy phrases to hurry past it. Say, 'This is heavy. I am angry. I am exhausted.' Honest naming invites God into your specificity—He already knows, but naming lets you bring Him the real thing. Look for the horizon, not the exit. Ask God to show one small way this pain might be shaping you—a softened word, a new boundary learned, a compassion born of pain. The horizon may simply be endurance that becomes ministry later, or a capacity to sit with someone else's grief." ~ Leslie Ginevra Montgomery[49]

When I write fiction, I know the outcome for my main

character. I'm the author. I know a happy ending is coming.

While writing one of my novels, my character was going through a terrible time. I wept for her as I wrote, begging her to hang in there and not give up. I knew she would be okay, and even though my character wasn't real, I still had empathy and concern.

God is the Author of Life. He knows the rest of your story. He weeps with you during your hard times. His heart aches when your heart aches. He brings comfort even though He knows you'll get a happy heavenly ending (which will actually be the most amazing beginning).

God knows you're going to be okay. You can trust Him.

> "If your heart feels split this season between gratitude and grief, hope and heaviness, you're not alone. God isn't asking you to fake it till you make it. He's inviting you to bring your full, authentic self—your tears, your praise, your doubts, your devotion—into His presence. Because He meets us not in the mask we wear, but in the truth we live. He is the Author who writes beauty into ashes, and sometimes the ink of redemption takes time to dry." ~ Leslie Ginevra Montgomery[50]

The story of what happened to Paul the apostle is found throughout the Bible. Although Paul faced terrible experiences, we recognize the effect his life had on those who learned the gospel from his travels. His life and the letters he wrote continue to have a profound impact on people.

Paul had rough times, but what a story, and what a life he led as he followed Christ. Can you imagine all the people who stepped into heaven because of Paul? They are still coming. Let's be like Paul, willing and ready to follow, serve, and obey our Master, Jesus, walking in God's will and God's way, no matter what may come.

> "He has chosen not to heal me, but to hold me. The more intense the pain, the closer His embrace." ~ Joni Eareckson Tada

"So we're not giving up. How could we! Even though on the outside it often looks like things are falling apart on us, on the inside, where God is making new life, not a day goes by without his unfolding grace. These hard times are small potatoes compared to the coming good times, the lavish celebration prepared for us. There's far more here than meets the eye. The things we see now are here today, gone tomorrow. But the things we can't see now will last forever," (2 Corinthians 4:16-18, MSG).

> "We can choose to gather to our hearts the thorns of disappointment, failure, loneliness, and dismay in our present situation. Or we can gather the flowers of God's grace, boundless love, abiding presence, and unmatched joy. I choose to gather the flowers." ~ Barbara Johnson

Beyond our present sufferings, God is working and moving. One day, we will witness the divine plan and be filled with joyful amazement and wonder.

> "I still believe that a day of understanding will come for each of us, however far away it may be. We will understand as we see the tragedies that today darken and dampen the presence of heaven for us to take their proper place in God's great plan—a plan so overwhelming, magnificent, and joyful, we will laugh with wonder and delight." ~ Arthur Christopher Bacon

Lisa Buffaloe

Tender boundaries

Have you ever wondered why you were born and why you lived in the places you did? God made from one man every nation of mankind to live on all the face of the earth, having determined allotted periods and the boundaries of their dwelling place, that they should seek God, and perhaps feel their way toward Him and find Him (Acts 17:26-27). God created each of us so that we would seek and find Him.

God set boundaries, placing us here and now for this time in history.

Where we are, where we have been, and even the difficulties in our lives all have an eternal purpose and plan.

> "Some things are so important to God that they are worth interrupting the happiness and health of His children in order to accomplish them." ~ Charles Stanley

God has placed each of us in the body of Christ to be used where He puts us in the body of Christ. He has plans and a purpose for each of us (1 Corinthians 12:18, Jeremiah 29:11).

My neck, hip, and back issues limit what I can do and where I can go. Life isn't what I expected.

I could once lift weights, take long walks with my husband, and work in our yard and garden. I loved traveling to see God's natural beauty. I miss being able to sleep and walk without hurting.

In the health-imposed isolation, I could be angry, pout, or whine. However, stress tightens my muscles, worsening the bulging discs and pinched nerves. Yet, besides praying for healing and seeking medical care, I wonder if there isn't a bigger purpose behind the pain.

I believe God has a plan, even now, and has called me to write. From morning until late afternoon (except for Sunday), I stand at my elevated desk, maintaining a fixed neck position as I write.

If I were as healthy and mobile as I used to be, would I be happy to spend most of my day at my desk writing, or would I prefer to be outside, traveling, socializing, and active?

For now, for this time, God has placed boundaries on my life.

I picture myself as a little sheep taken from the pasture and placed in a pen in the barn. The other sheep and lambs are playing and running around in the green grass, and here I am stuck inside.

Yet, when I stop and consider, I notice my boundaries may be restricted, yet they are tender with God's love.

The Psalmist wrote, "The boundary lines have fallen for me in pleasant places; indeed, I have a beautiful inheritance," (Psalm 16:6, HCSB).

Joni Eareckson Tada was an active teenager when a diving accident in 1967 left her paralyzed from the shoulders down. Joni struggled with depression and anger, and she even considered ending her life as she grappled with her faith, wondering how God could let the tragedy occur.

God met Joni in the midst of her pain and questions. Despite her situation, a determination was birthed to help others with similar disabilities.

> "The best we can hope for in this life is a knothole peek at the shining realities ahead. Yet a glimpse is enough. It's enough to convince our hearts that whatever sufferings and sorrows currently assail us aren't worthy of comparison to that which waits over the horizon." ~ Joni Eareckson Tada

Though paralyzed and restricted to a wheelchair, Joni's

Christian organization, her writing, speaking, and artwork, provide programs and services for thousands of special needs families around the world.

> "God's hands stay on the wheel of your life from start to finish so that everything follows his intention for your life. This means your trials have more meaning—much more—than you realize."
> ~ Joni Eareckson Tada

Are you restricted by health or circumstances?

The Apostle Paul penned many letters while either imprisoned or confined to house arrest.

> "Circumstances may appear to wreck our lives and God's plans, but God is not helpless among ruins. Our broken lives are not lost or useless. God's love is still working. He comes in and takes the calamity and uses it victoriously, working out his plan of love."
> ~ Eric Liddell

Paul wrote to the Philippians from prison, stating that his situation had, in fact, furthered the gospel, making it known to the entire palace guard. Also, Paul wrote that his Christian brethren became confident and fearlessly proclaimed the message of Christ.

Other letters Paul wrote were also written during times of confinement, yet God worked through Paul in mighty ways.

"Therefore, we do not become discouraged (utterly spiritless, exhausted, and wearied out through fear). Though our outer man is [progressively] decaying and wasting away, yet our inner self is being [progressively] renewed day after day. For our light, momentary affliction (this slight distress of the passing hour) is ever more and more abundantly preparing and producing and achieving for us an everlasting weight of glory [beyond all measure, excessively surpassing all comparisons and all calculations, a vast and transcendent glory and blessedness never to cease!], (2

Corinthians 4:16-17, AMPC).

As a Christian, the ending will be amazing. However, until then, life can be terribly painful. Regardless of our level of faith, we will encounter problems.

> "The question is often asked, 'Why is human life drenched in so much blood and soaked with so many tears?' The answer is found in the word 'achieving,' for these 'momentary troubles are achieving for us' something very precious. They are teaching us not only the way to victory but, better still, the law of victory—there is a reward for every sorrow, and the sorrow itself produces the reward." ~ L. B. Cowman[51]

In his second letter to Timothy, Paul wrote, At my first defense, no one stood by me, but everyone deserted me. But the Lord stood with me and strengthened me" (2 Timothy 4:16-17, HCSB).

People may fail us, but God never will.

> "Remember that Christ, in His gentle sustaining help, comes near to us all across the sea of sorrow and trouble. A more tender, a more gracious sense of His nearness to us is ever granted to us in the time of our darkness and our grief than is possible to us in the sunny hours of joy. It is always the stormy sea that Christ comes across, to draw near to us; and those who have never experienced the tempest have yet to learn the inmost sweetness of His presence. When it is night, and it is dark, at the hour that is the keystone of night's black arch, Christ comes to us, striding across the stormy waters. The storm is not as real as the Christ. The waves will pass, but He abides forever. Take Christ on board and let Him stand between you and the tempest."
> ~ Alexander Maclaren

After improper medical treatment when she was six weeks old,

Fanny Crosby lost her sight.

Some would have said Fanny was handicapped because of her blindness. She said her blindness was a blessing.

Inspiring words seemed to flow constantly from Fanny Crosby's heart, and she wrote over 8,000 gospel texts and hymns. Though blind, she described herself as "the happiest creature in all the land."

A man once mentioned to Fanny that it was such a pity she had been born blind. Her immediate response was that she would have wished to be born without sight, so that upon entering heaven, the first face she would see would be that of her Savior.

Fanny Crosby was physically blind, but her spiritual eyesight was exceptional. Her eyes couldn't see, but her soul sang.

Beyond earthly sight, God is working.

> "Extraordinary afflictions are not always the punishment of extraordinary sins but are sometimes the trials resulting from God's extraordinary gifts." ~ Charles Spurgeon

Never limit what He can do, and is doing, in our life or the lives of others, for a glorious end is coming.

> "We have to be faithful in the small things. We're so obsessed with oceans and mighty floods that we forget that little ripples of faith, hope, and love can change the world." ~ Eugene Cho

A story is told of a small Dutch boy who noticed water trickling through a crack in the levee. He realized the danger and plugged the leaking levee with his finger. He was only a little boy, yet because he was there, present in the moment, his action saved the village from flooding.

What if the little boy had been too busy looking at social media or the news? What if he was upset at the levee's problems and complained instead of fixing the problem?

In Ezekiel 22:30, we read that God searched for someone to build a wall and stand in the gap before Him for the land, so that He would not destroy it, but He found no one.

The enemy wants us to stay so busy and distracted by what is going on in our lives, or around us, that we aren't paying attention to where God has placed us and the calling He has for us.

The world is leaking; the dam is bursting, because many are not standing in the gap before the Lord and being faithful where God placed them.

Within the boundaries of your life, be faithful where you are.

> "God breathed His life into you. You are exceptional, and exceptional people sometimes face exceptional difficulties. But the good news is we serve an exceptional God! You may face many defeats in your life, but never let yourself be defeated. Keep standing in faith, keep declaring victory over your future, and keep declaring the promises of God over your life. Keep declaring that you are moving forward into the bright, exceptional tomorrow that the Lord has in store for you!" ~ Mark Evans

Our back porch is adorned with flowers growing in various pots. We enjoy either sitting on our porch or admiring the lovely flowers from the breakfast room.

What if the flowers longed to be in the yard rather than in a container and became angry at their circumstances, refusing to bloom?

How much would the plants miss?

They'd miss the protection of being in a pot safe from the harsh sun's rays and the downpour of rain. They'd miss the joy of blooming beautiful flowers, of seeing our smiles, the joy of happy bees, butterflies, and hummingbirds. They'd miss pleasing the one who planted them.

They'd miss joy.

Where have you been planted?

Are you angry at your situation, or will you bloom for the Lord?

> "Take the very hardest thing in your life—the place of difficulty, outward or inward—and expect God to triumph gloriously in that very spot. Just there, He can bring your soul into blossom."
> ~ Lilias Trotter

In the difficulties, in the shadows of life, within the boundaries where you have been placed, God is working in wonderful ways.

Please don't miss the opportunity to bloom for God where you have been planted.

Praise power

A friend emailed her prayer partners and suggested we take a few days not to ask God for anything, but instead spend that time thanking and praising Him.

I wondered what that would look like? How could that be done when there are so many needs?

Then I thought of a friend I often visited. I know she loved me and was glad to see me. However, whenever I went to her house, she would happily talk with me, but the TV usually stayed on, and she would stay busy cleaning and doing things around her home.

There wasn't a moment of silence where we could sit together, talk in a quiet environment, and enjoy one another's company.

Another friend never calls unless she has a problem. She has never called to tell me anything good in her life. Instead, her calls have been complaints, worries, and concerns. Then she would ask me to pray for her, and off she would go with her life.

I wondered, have I been that kind of friend to God?

Even during prayer, I've stayed busy and distracted. I've called on God over and over with my complaints, worries, and concerns, then trotted off to go about my day.

How often have I come into God's presence just to say hello, tell Him I love Him, thank Him for who He is, and all He has done, and sit quietly, waiting and listening?

I want to do better—to change my prayers so they bless and honor God.

> "I strongly suspect that if we saw all the difference even the tiniest of our prayers make, all the people those little prayers were destined to affect, and all the consequences of those prayers down through the centuries, we would be so paralyzed with awe at the power of prayer that we would be unable to get up off our knees for the rest of our lives." ~ Peter Kreeft

The wonderful thing is that even with our real-life concerns, we can pray in a spirit of praise and thanksgiving. This doesn't always come easily, especially during life's difficulties. Yet, we are told to offer God the sacrifice of thanksgiving and that the one who offers a sacrifice of praise and thanksgiving honors God.

> "God isn't asking you to be thankful. He's asking you to give thanks. There's a big difference. One response involves emotions; the other your choices, your decisions about a situation, your intent, your 'step of faith." ~ Joni Eareckson Tada[52]

How do we offer thanks?

One way is flipping our worries, concerns, and complaints into praise and thanksgiving. When we do, the more peace floods the soul, the more encouragement (and courage) is given, the stronger our hope becomes, and the more our faith grows.

> "Praise is rooted not in the circumstances of the moment but in the nature and trustworthiness of God."
> ~ Henry and Richard Blackaby[53]

If family members or friends are lost and have strayed from God, we can still praise God because He desires no one perish, nothing is impossible for Him, and He loves more than we can imagine. Praise God that He searches for lost sheep and finds them, and His mercies are new every morning.

During painful health issues, we can praise God that He is the

Great Physician who heals, restores, redeems, and will help us with whatever health problem we face.

> "Yes, I pray that my pain might be removed, that it might cease; but more so, I pray for the strength to bear it, the grace to benefit from it, and the devotion to offer it up to God as a sacrifice of praise." ~ Joni Eareckson Tada

During sleepless nights, praise God that He is always available. In the morning, we can praise God for any sleep we received.

In times of financial difficulty, praise God, who owns everything and promises to provide us with all we truly need.

When lonely, praise God that He is with us 24/7 and will never leave or forsake us.

Whatever you're facing, whatever worry and concern you may have, whatever burden you may carry, thank and praise God that He is loving and compassionate, and all things are possible for Him.

When the world seems out of control, praise God that He is always in control and His plans and purpose will prevail. Thank God that, for those who love the Lord, He turns what the enemy meant for evil into good.

When bad things happen and evil seems to win, praise God, that He is righteous and just, and evil will be punished.

When happy, praise God.

When struggling, when life beats you bloody, praise God because, in Christ, you will always get an incredible, happy, joyful, eternal ending.

Praise and thanksgiving are God-given, powerful gifts.

> "Praise pierces the darkness, dynamites long-standing obstructions, and sends the demons of hell fleeing. Praise is the Christian's heavy artillery; praise is more effective in spiritual warfare than is an atom bomb in military battle." ~ Wesley Duewel

2 Chronicles recounts that a gigantic army was coming against the country of Judah. King Jehoshaphat sought the Lord, proclaimed a fast, and prayed.

With an interesting plan of attack, their little army assembled, and those who were to sing to the Lord and praise him were in holy attire and went before the army, saying, "Give thanks to the Lord, for His steadfast love endures forever."

<u>When they began to sing and praise</u>, the Lord set an ambush against those who had come against Judah, and their enemy was routed.

Praising God releases the power of God.

> "Praise focuses on God, not the circumstance, and fixes its gaze upon God's truth and God's character instead of the trial at hand or just ahead. That is why we can celebrate the battle before it begins. The outcome is neither our responsibility nor our goal. Praise begins and ends with faith in the very nature, personality, and integrity of God, and that never changes." ~ Mary Southerland

Acts 16:16-31 records that Paul and Silas were beaten with rods, thrown in the inner prison, and their feet fastened in stocks. Despite the unjust treatment and immense suffering these men endured, Luke tells us that Paul and Silas were praying and singing hymns to God around midnight, and the other prisoners were listening.

Paul and Silas knew something many people do not understand. They were prepared for life's difficulties and enemy attacks by remembering the power of prayer and praise.

> Prayer "surmounts or removes all obstacles, overcomes every resisting force, and gains its ends in the face of invincible hindrances." ~ E. M. Bounds

Singing scripture, praying scripture gives power, for there is power in the word of God, for His word never returns void and is truth and life.

When we pray, when we sing and pray scripture, it releases God's power and feeds our souls.

Praising God lifts our eyes from our problems to our all-powerful, eternal-loving God.

> "Praise is the switch that turns on the light of joy in our lives, even when it's 'dark' outside. And the resulting 'light' causes others to see the glory of God in our lives." ~ Anne Graham Lotz

We don't know what Paul and Silas were praying and singing while they were in jail, but we know God's power fell. Suddenly, the prison's foundations shook because of a violent earthquake. Every door swung open, and every person's chains came off.

There is GREAT power in prayer and praise beyond what we can imagine or conceive.

Through prayer and praise, God can bring about change, break down barriers, and release those imprisoned. When we praise and pray, we find freedom, and this sparks a ripple effect, freeing those around us. According to Philippians 4:6-7, praying with thanks offers peace, safeguarding our hearts and minds.

Paul and Silas were praying and praising God by singing hymns. Most likely, the men were singing scripture, perhaps from the Psalms.

No matter how your voice sounds, whether or not you can carry a tune, there is power in singing hymns and speaking and praising using God's word.

Quote scripture out loud, sing praises, use your voice to speak words of life and truth.

There is life-giving power in God's beautiful word on the substance of our being as we praise and pray.

> "No matter what difficult times we encounter, God is worthy of our praise. When we choose to praise, we choose to trust God. When we choose to trust God, the broken world around us lifts their eyebrows in wonder. Sometimes a sacrifice of praise is required. Offer it. We can and should choose to bless His name through the pain, which, astonishingly, can bring His joy into our hearts." ~ Gwen Smith[54]

When Paul and Silas prayed and sang hymns, God moved, chains fell off, prison doors opened, and yet the prisoners remained in their cells. God placed a holy hush, a holy pause on that jail and the prisoners, because God had more planned.

When the jailer discovered the cell doors opened, he assumed everyone had escaped, drew his sword, and was going to kill himself. But Paul called out in a loud voice, "Don't harm yourself, because all of us are here!"

The jailer asked for torches, rushed in, and fell trembling before Paul and Silas. Then he escorted them out and asked, What must I do to be saved?

Paul and Silas replied, "Believe in the Lord Jesus, and you will be saved, you and your household. And they spoke the word of the Lord to him and to all who were in his house."

The jailer and each member of his household accepted Christ as their Savior. Can you imagine the joy as each person realized that Jesus Christ died for their sins and that they had a merciful, forgiving Savior?

God moved in wonderful ways, but the disciples still suffered.

Sometimes God protects us from difficulties, and sometimes God protects us through problems. He promises, "I will be with you when you pass through the waters, and when you pass through the rivers, they will not overwhelm you. You will not be scorched when you walk through the fire, and the flame will not burn you," (Isaiah 43:2, HCSB).

"The one who offers thanksgiving as his sacrifice glorifies Me;

to one who orders his way rightly I will show the salvation of God!" (Psalm 50:23, ESV).

Sometimes, thanksgiving and praising God *are* sacrifices.

Paul wrote about the hardships he and the early Christians faced, yet they were sorrowful but rejoicing (2 Corinthians 6:10).

Despite my ongoing neck issues, I remain joyful and thankful to God for the many parts of my body that function painlessly.

"Through Him, therefore, let us constantly and at all times offer up to God a sacrifice of praise, which is the fruit of lips that thankfully acknowledge and confess and glorify His name (Hebrews 13:15, AMPC).

"We can hug our hurts and make a shrine out of our sorrows, or we can offer them to God as a sacrifice of praise. The choice is ours."
~ Richard Exley

I'm choosing to offer a sacrifice of praise to God.

Will you join me?

Let's enter His gates with thanksgiving and into His courts with praise! Be thankful and bless and affectionately praise His name! For the Lord is good; His mercy and loving-kindness are everlasting; His faithfulness and truth endure to all generations (Psalm 100:3-5).

"In the silent times, seek God. In the painful times, praise God. In the terrible times, trust God. And at all times, and at all times, thank God." ~ Ann Voskamp

---

"Hallelujah! Praise God in His sanctuary. Praise Him in His mighty heavens. Praise Him for His powerful acts; praise Him for His abundant greatness. Praise Him with trumpet blast; praise Him with harp and lyre. Praise Him with tambourine and dance; praise Him with flute and strings. Praise Him with resounding cymbals; praise Him with clashing cymbals. Let everything that breathes praise the Lord. Hallelujah!" (Psalm 150, HCSB)

> "O God, my heart pants for Thee as David's of old did. I long to know Thee in all the beauty of Thy self-revelation and in all of Thy perfection. The way into Thy heart may be difficult and treacherous, but I can bear the difficulties as long as I discover in them the fullness of Thy character and nature. Amen."
> ~ A. W. Tozer[55]

Moving forward

Before my mobility was limited, my fitness tracker recorded my steps, calories, and other information to help me stay healthy. Knowing my movements were scrutinized made me more active.

It was fun seeing how I was doing each day, especially when the monitor buzzed with excitement at reaching a set goal. However, if the tracker was off my wrist, I felt like any steps taken were wasted. I wanted to get credit when I moved.

How do we find freedom in our daily walk?

My Biblical hero walker is Enoch (Genesis 5:24). Enoch lived a devoted life, walked so closely with God that, before he died, God took him home to heaven.

Enoch didn't waste a single step.

> "So much of the journey forward involves a letting go of all that once brought us life. We turn away from the familiar abiding places of the heart, the false selves we have lived out, the strengths we have used to make a place for ourselves and all our false loves, and we venture forth in our hearts to trace the steps of the One who said, 'Follow me.'" ~ John Eldredge

Emma Gatewood, known as Grandma Gatewood, was an American hiking pioneer. She faced hardship as a farm wife, a mother to eleven, and a victim of domestic violence.

In 1955, at the age of sixty-seven, Grandma Gatewood achieved the distinction of being the first woman to hike the 2,168-mile Appalachian Trail.

Wearing canvas Keds shoes on her misshapen feet, she took little in the way of outdoor gear. No tent or sleeping bag, just a shower curtain to keep the rain off, a small notebook, some clothes, and food in a homemade denim bag slung over one shoulder.

Emma endured hardships and difficulties during her walk, but she didn't stop. Grandma Gatewood had a walking goal, and she didn't give up; she kept walking.

What is your spiritual walking goal?

> "Live every day to fulfill your personal mission. God has a reason for whatever season you are living through right now. A season of loss or blessing? A season of activity or hibernation? A season of growth or incubation? You may think you're on a detour, but God knows the best way for you to reach your destination."
> ~ Barbara Johnson[56]

Whether facing health issues, circumstances, or other challenges, we can still walk with God. Because no matter how confined we are physically, our souls are always free.

> "There comes a time for each of us when merely talking about the Christian pilgrimage is not sufficient. We must actually set out on the journey! We can spend many hours debating and discussing issues related to the Christian life, but this means little if we never actually step out and follow Christ! Christianity is not a set of teachings to understand. It is a Person to follow."
> ~ Henry & Richard Blackaby[57]

Have you ever watched sheep and their shepherd? Sheep follow; they don't know where they are going, yet they follow their shepherd.

Sheep don't sit and analyze where he might lead or if there is another way. They trust their shepherd and follow.

Abram was called to leave his country and his people and to follow God, without knowing where God would lead. Abram didn't question; he packed up and followed.

Jesus called His disciples without telling them where they were going, and they followed.

Not knowing where they were going, they followed.

> "The Bible is full of ordinary people who went to impossible places and did wondrous things simply because they decided to follow Jesus." ~ Brother Andrew

God uses ordinary, flawed men and women who step out in obedience to accomplish His perfect purpose.

Peter, after Jesus' crucifixion and resurrection, stood firm, fearlessly speaking the truth about Jesus and sharing the gospel with a large crowd.

Considering Peter's past actions—fleeing during Jesus' arrest, denying Him, and hiding after His death—how did he become brave enough to confront those who crucified Jesus Christ?

Peter told the truth because He knew the One who is Truth. His transformation was because of the presence and influence of the risen Lord's Spirit within him. Peter was now operating under the influence of God's Holy Spirit, equipping and empowering him, helping him speak, and reminding him of everything Jesus said and did. Peter went from wavering self-confidence to soul-deep God-confidence.

Peter now understood Jesus was the risen Lord, who has all authority in heaven and earth and is seated at the right hand of God, interceding for those who are His.

Peter understood his mission to go, tell, make disciples, feed

Christ's sheep, and spread the good news to all nations. Peter got it, and as believers in Christ, I want us to get it too.

Let's remember the truth about who Christ is, who we are in Christ, and the power and equipping we receive through the Holy Spirit, who provides guidance, wisdom, and helps us understand God's word.

That's the beauty of Bible study. The more time spent reading the Bible, the more we learn about who God really is; His mercy flows out, His love swirls from the pages to engulf and guide us. The more we read and study the Bible, the more we understand who Jesus is and how we can best follow Him.

> "When Jesus walked among humankind, there was a certain simplicity to being his disciple. Primarily, it meant to go with him, in an attitude of observation, study, obedience, and imitation. There were no correspondence courses. Disciples had to be with him to learn how to do what he did." ~ Dallas Willard[58]

As followers of Christ, we can turn away from our lack of confidence, our own inadequacies, failures, and fears, and rest confidently in our all-powerful God and His all-sufficient Holy Spirit.

> "Pray to Jesus to make you all you can be. Say to Him, 'Use me to the fullness of my capability. Touch my silent tongue, equip my idle hands, and open my frostbitten wallet. Send a full stream of life upon me that all my soul may wake up, and all that is within me may adore you. Get out of me all that can possibly come out of such a poor thing as I am. Let your Spirit work in me to the praise of the glory of your grace.' Oh, for men and women who are alive from head to foot, whose entire existence is full of consecration to Jesus and zeal for the divine glory; these have life 'to the full'"
> ~ Charles Spurgeon

If we don't step out of our comfort zone, over our problems, in line with God, through (or around) whatever fear/good thing/bad thing that holds us back, and follow God's ways, what will we miss?

I want nothing to hold me back (especially me) from following God.

> "The choices you make when you feel God's nudge will become the hinges on which your destiny swings. Each individual decision you make, to obey or ignore God's promptings and directives, is a thread that weaves the tapestry of your life." ~ Sharon Jaynes[59]

Through the journey of life, I don't want to wander or miss a moment. I don't want to miss God's best.

> "If I am going to experience a greater measure of God's power in my life, it will usually involve the first-step principle. It will usually begin by my acting in faith—trusting God enough to take a step of obedience." ~ John Ortberg[60]

I would prefer the ability to see the road ahead, or have a roadmap, or a book I could open each morning that would tell me what I need to accomplish that day. I could even skip to the ending and read about my happily ever after in God's presence.

However, if I had a to-do list for each moment, would my rebellious nature rebel? Would I be obedient if I didn't like everything on the list? Would I get so caught up in anticipating and preparing for the future that I'd neglect my current duties? Furthermore, my idea of preparation might differ completely from God's plan.

The journey requires trust.

Without knowing what is next or where He leads, Jesus invites us to follow Him—trusting Him with the process and the future.

> "Never be afraid to trust an unknown future to a known God."
> ~ Corrie Ten Boom

Only God knows the future. Only He knows what's ahead.

> "Does it matter where you are going as long as you are going with God? What if we changed our destination goals — so that God is the goal? The goal isn't a place — the goal is a Person. The goal is the Presence of your Provider, your Peace, your Purpose, your Person. . . . your Jesus. The goal isn't walking to somewhere as much as it is walking with Someone. God is the goal."
> - Ann Voskamp[61]

Paul wrote that as Christians, we are to run our race, fight the good fight, and run to win. For most of my life, I assumed that meant I should stay busy — always busy. If I wasn't busy doing something for the Lord, I wasn't running well; I was a slacker, not a dutiful servant.

I finally realized Paul wasn't always on the go; there were times he stayed in one town and ministered where God placed him.

Jesus went from town to town doing good, but also took time to rest and pray. In all things there is a season, and a time for every purpose under heaven (Ecclesiastes 3:1).

> "One reason we are so harried and hurried is that we make yesterday and tomorrow our business, when all that legitimately concerns us is today. If we really have too much to do, there are some items on the agenda which God did not put there. Let us submit the list to Him and ask Him to indicate which items we must delete. There is always time to do the will of God. If we are too busy to do that, we are too busy." ~ Elisabeth Elliot[62]

In Luke 10, we read that Martha was busy and frustrated with meal preparation, upset that Mary wasn't helping.

And yet, Jesus told Mary that Mary had chosen the better thing—the one thing that mattered (Luke 10:38-42). And that one thing is sitting at the feet of Christ.

> "When life can easily be pulled apart and when so many voices tell us what to do, we need to be like Mary and keep our priorities straight. We must make time daily to sit at the feet of Jesus, listen to his Word, and receive truth that is good, needful, and lasting. If we do this, we will please the Lord. There is a time for being a servant like Martha, but it is important that we first take time for worshiping, loving, and learning at the feet of Jesus. This is true preparation for acceptable service." ~ Warren Wiersbe [63]

Have we sat at the feet of Jesus?

Jesus said to love the Lord your God with all your heart, soul, mind, and strength.

> "God so loved the world that He gave ... no end, no time limit, no measure, no calculation. His giving could only be called a reckless abandonment of love. Do I love Him in like measure, and am I willing to show it by a similar reckless abandonment?"
> ~ Helen Roseveare

Many people claim to love God; however, merely saying the words is not enough. If we truly love God, we will obey Him. When we cherish God, our love and passion for Him grows, and we want to spend time with Him and please Him.

Love calls for action, and obedience is the sign of love.

When we love someone, we want to do things for them and spend time with them.

Jesus said, If you really love Me, you will keep and obey My commandments. Those who follow My instructions and abide by them are those who truly love Me, and My Father will love those who genuinely love Me; I will also love them and reveal Myself to them. I will let Myself be clearly seen by him and make myself real to them. If you obey my commands, you will remain in my love, just as I have obeyed my Father's commands and remained in His love (John 14:15, 14:21, John 15:10).

> "As the world tries to persuade people to follow its standard, your life should stand in stark contrast as an example of a righteous person. Your life would convince those around you of the wisdom of following God. Do not underestimate the positive effect that your obedience will have upon those close to you."
> ~ Henry & Richard Blackaby[64]

If we really love God and love His Son, Jesus Christ, we will be obedient to His commands.

> "The Gospels call us to obedience, not as an optional extra, but as a basic requirement for all who would follow Christ."
> ~ Helen Roseveare[65]

True Christianity is more than lip service; it is a life dedicated to following and obeying Christ.

> "Obedience prepares the mind for revelation, takes from that revelation the light that dazzles the spirit's vision and prepares the heart to receive wider demonstrations of the grace of God."
> ~ Joseph Parker[66]

As we love and obey God, we have the incredible opportunity to be loved by God and to receive more knowledge and understanding.

Every step taken in obedience leads to the blessings of God.

When I was a teenager, my dad asked me to clean the kitchen. I spent a few minutes wiping down the surfaces, doing what I believed was a decent job.

My dad came back and asked if I was certain I had thoroughly cleaned the kitchen. I assured him I had. Without saying a word, Dad moved a canister that had been on the counter. Underneath was a five-dollar bill.

Because of my half-hearted effort, I missed the blessing.

> "When we follow God's direction, we will witness things happening in our lives that can only be explained by His powerful presence. How could we be satisfied with anything less?"
> ~ Henry & Richard Blackaby[67]

I made a promise to God that I would go anywhere at any time He wished. However, sometimes an offer to move forward came, and I whimpered and held back, my fear and insecurity causing me to hesitate.

> "If my relationship to God is that of love, I will do what He says without hesitation. If I hesitate, it is because I love someone I have placed in competition with Him, namely, myself. Jesus Christ will not force me to obey Him, but I must. And as soon as I obey Him, I fulfill my spiritual destiny. My personal life may be crowded with small, petty happenings, altogether insignificant. But if I obey Jesus Christ in the seemingly random circumstances of life, they become pinholes through which I see the face of God. When God's redemption brings a human soul to the point of obedience, it always produces. If I obey Jesus Christ, the redemption of God will flow through me to the lives of others, because behind the deed of obedience is the reality of Almighty God." ~ Oswald Chambers[68]

Through obedience, our understanding deepens, and God provides more opportunities to experience His divine actions and operations.

> "On your own journey, can you dare to ask God for something really different? Unusual? Wonderful? Unique? I can't promise you He will do it, but I do know that when we leave our choices with Him, He frequently takes us off the beaten thoroughfare and the woods to watch the snow fall, or through a shop door to meet a new friend, or down a rough path toward a treasure at the end, or even into His waiting arms that will ultimately give us peace."
> ~ Luci Swindoll [69]

To live free in Christ, please don't miss the absolutely amazing blessing of following, loving, and obeying God.

Finding Freedom in a Binding World

Guard your heart and strengthen the core

> "If you can't name specific ways you are taking care of your heart, then it is probably in need of attention." ~ Allen Arnold

We lock the doors of our houses and cars. We set alarms to stay safe. Are we as diligent in guarding our hearts?

"Keep and guard your heart with all vigilance and above all that you guard, for out of it flow the springs of life." (Proverbs 4:23, AMPC)

There is a constant gravitational pull to the things of this earth. I catch myself wondering what's happening, so I'll jump online to check social media. The more the world distracts, the more powerful the hold becomes and the more bound I feel.

Yet when I spend time with God in prayer, Bible study, or the precious moments of being still in God's presence, the lighter and freer I feel, and the less attached I am to the things of the world.

To experience the freedom that Christ offers, we must be intentional about protecting our hearts from harmful influences.

> "At the heart of Jesus' teachings are these truths: Make room in your life to care for your soul. Protect it. Guard it."
> ~ John Ortberg [70]

Take a mental health break, step away from the news and social media. Our hearts are constantly under attack. The enemy wants to diminish our passion for Christ and weaken our spiritual resolve.

> "Faith never finds her wisdom in the thoughts of men or in pretended revelations, but she resorts to the inspired Word of God for her guidance. This is the well from which she drinks, the manna on which she feeds. Faith takes the Lord Jesus to be her wisdom. The knowledge of Christ is to her the most excellent of the sciences. Jesus Christ is the Alpha and Omega of the Bible. He is the constant theme of its sacred pages; from first to last, they testify of Him (see John 5:39)." ~ Charles Spurgeon

Just as physical health depends on a strong core, our spiritual well-being relies on a disciplined and strong inner life. Without conscious effort, our faith can become vulnerable, susceptible to confusion and discouragement.

Freedom in Christ is not passive; it requires a commitment to spiritual health.

> "In God's Word, we not only discover His will for our lives, we find words of genuine comfort for those times when life is unglued." ~ Chuck Swindoll

Reading and meditating on God's Word renews our minds, equips us to discern truth, brings comfort and guidance, guards against the enemy's lies, and strengthens our spiritual core.

While on this earth, we live in enemy territory, and many of our restless struggles come from external forces. Satan is out to steal, kill, and destroy.

Peter warned us that the devil prowls around like a roaring lion seeking someone to devour.

Our struggle is not against flesh and blood. Paul said to put on the whole armor of God so we can stand against the schemes of the devil and the spiritual forces of darkness.

God never leaves us defenseless in our battles. The Bible is our offensive weapon—the sword of the Spirit.

> "Herein is true wisdom. If you would successfully wrestle with Satan, make the Holy Scriptures your daily resort. Out of this sacred magazine, continually draw your armor and your ammunition. Lay hold upon the glorious doctrines of God's Word; make them your daily meat and drink. So shall you be strong to resist the devil, and you shall be joyful in discovering that he will flee from you." ~ Charles Spurgeon

As we read and study, the Holy Spirit illuminates and opens our minds to understand things hidden from the foundation of the world. The Bible is alive, powerful, active, energizing, equipping, training, correcting, instructing, renewing, and restoring our minds and souls.

Study the Old and New Testaments. I often read a chronological Bible that helps bring clarity and order to the Biblical accounts.

> "The Old Testament is the cradle in which the Christ child is laid."
> ~ Martin Luther

Every part of Scripture is inspired by God and is beneficial for teaching, correcting wrongdoing, setting things right, and guiding people to live in a way that pleases God.

> "A Bible that's falling apart usually belongs to someone who isn't."
> ~ Charles Spurgeon

Therefore, "Do not be conformed to this present world, but be transformed by the renewing of your mind, so that you may test and approve what is the will of God—what is good and well-pleasing and perfect. Making "every effort to present yourself before God as a proven worker who does not need to be ashamed, teaching the message of truth accurately. (Matthew 4:4, Hebrews 4:12, AMPC; 2 Timothy 3:16-17, AMP; Romans 12:2, 2 Timothy 2:15; NET)

For your freedom and protection, guard your heart, and keep your spiritual core strong by staying updated in God's word.

Wait well

Waiting isn't easy. Waiting for prayers to be answered, for change to come, for the prodigal to return home, for healing, for financial help ... waiting.

I've offered lengthy, heartfelt, begging prayers for years in several matters, imploring God for help. But I'm still waiting. I don't understand why, but I will continue to wait, pray, and believe.

There are days when I'm strong, faith-filled, and content. Other days, not so much. Patience is difficult.

> "Patience is the ability to idle your motor when you feel like stripping your gears." ~ Barbara Johnson

I'm not a fan of waiting. Yet delays aren't always negative. If I want something, I prefer it as soon as possible. However, if I'm crossing a river full of crocodiles, I would be delighted to delay until any large-tooth critters are gone or occupied with something else.

> "Waiting on God requires the willingness to bear uncertainty, to carry within oneself the unanswered question, lifting the heart to God about it whenever it intrudes upon one's thoughts."
> ~ Elisabeth Elliot

Even though prayers remain unanswered, even though I do not understand, I need to continue doing what God has called me to do and keep focused on the Lord.

I'm waiting, and I want to wait well.

Beyond human sight, God is working. Our stops and delays are often a preparation, a getting rid of the things not needed for the next part of our journey, a soul-stilling that tunes the soul to God, preparing us for what God has planned.

> "Faith will find its strength, not in the thought of what you will or do, but in the unchanging faithfulness and love of Christ, who has assured you once again that those who wait on Him will not be ashamed." ~ Andrew Murray

Throughout the Bible, people had to wait.

Noah waited and worked for decades, building the ark, and then spent another 370 days inside the huge boat. Abraham waited for his promised child.

Elijah waited three years in isolation. Joseph was sold into slavery and then imprisoned and had to wait thirteen years for God's promises. Moses spent forty years in the desert. David, though anointed king over Israel, had to wait years for that promise to happen.

Jesus waited thirty years before beginning His ministry.

Yet after the waiting, amazing things happened — a baby born to elderly parents, a nation returned to God, a prominent position in a kingdom given, people rescued from bondage, seas parted, enemies defeated, promises brought to fruition, the dead brought back to life, and salvation offered to all who will believe.

> "The Lord is always punctual. He never keeps His servants waiting one single tick of the clock beyond His own appointed, fitting, wise, and proper moment." ~ Charles Spurgeon

Illness and surgeries have often caused me to slow down, stop, and wait. Those times were the worst of times and the best of times. They were hard, horribly painful, yet came with beautiful blessings.

When all you can do is spend time with The One who made you, that time is good, very good.

Sometimes a delay is because of the actions of others.

Joshua and Caleb were among those who scouted the land God promised to the Israelites. Even though the land was beautiful and perfect, only those two men gave a good report and believed God would help them take the land.

Because of the rest of the nation's unbelief in God's ability to help them take the land, the nation wandered in the desert for forty years. Joshua and Caleb waited to enter the promised land because of the actions of other people.

Yet God rewarded those long, hard years of waiting, and Caleb was blessed, and Joshua led the Israelites into the promised land.

> George Mueller made a note in his Bible next to Psalm 37:23 "The steps of a good man are ordered by the Lord. And the stops, too. It is a sad mistake to break through God's hedges. It is a vital principle of the Lord's guidance for a Christian never to move from the spot where he is sure God has placed him until the 'pillar of cloud' (Ex. 13:21) moves." ~ L. B. Cowman

Jesus commanded His disciples not to leave Jerusalem, but to wait for what the Father had promised (Acts 1:4). The disciples didn't know how long they had to wait — twenty-four hours or twenty-four years in a city that had just crucified their Savior and remained very hostile to those who professed to be Christians. Yet, Jesus told them to wait.

In God's perfect timing, the Holy Spirit fell on the followers of Jesus Christ. The resurrection power of the indwelling Spirit came to work in them to be His witnesses to the ends of the earth.

> "When you are 'in the wait' period, I like to think I'm enclosed in the parentheses of God's arms of love." ~ George Wesley Dixon

Isn't that a beautiful thought?

God promises in Isaiah 40:31 that those "who wait for the Lord shall renew their strength; they shall mount up with wings like eagles; they shall run and not be weary; they shall walk and not faint."

> "The word renew in Isaiah 40:31 actually means 'exchange.' They that wait upon the Lord shall exchange their strength. We exchange our strength for His strength. We hand in our little pocket batteries and plug into His dynamo!" ~ Warren Wiersbe[71]

I love that visual. I need to remember when I am weak and so tired of waiting to take my little pocket batteries and plug into God's dynamic power.

The Passion Translation of Isaiah 40:31 reads, "Those who entwine their hearts with Yahweh will experience divine strength. They will rise up on soaring wings and fly like eagles, run their race without growing weary, and walk through life without giving up."

As we wait on the Lord, our hearts entwine with the Lord. Oh, what an amazing reality!

> "Faith will find its strength, not in the thought of what you will or do, but in the unchanging faithfulness and love of Christ, who has assured you once again that those who wait on Him will not be ashamed." ~ Andrew Murray

Are you waiting? The unchanging faithfulness and love of Christ will never fail.

"The Lord takes delight in his faithful followers, and in those who wait for his loyal love. Wait for the Lord; be strong and let your heart take courage; yes, wait for the Lord. For the Lord God is a sun and shield; the Lord gives grace and glory; no good thing does He withhold from those who walk uprightly," (Psalm 147:11, NET; Psalm

27:14, NASB; Psalm 84:11, NASB).

> "The Spirit requires not only a service of work but also a service of waiting. I cannot see that in the kingdom of Christ, there are not only times for action but times to refrain from action."
> ~ George Matheson

In your waiting, stay your soul on God. Be still. Rest and know, you are always safe in God's hands.

Be still, wait patiently (Psalm 37:7).

Be still and know that He is God (Psalm 46:10).

Be still; He calms the storm (Mark 4:39)

Be still; the Lord rescues; the Lord fights for His children (Exodus 14:14).

We don't have to know the future, but we can rest easy knowing our timeless God has all of time in His loving hands.

> "You can save a lot of time by waiting on God." ~ Adrian Rogers

Wait and watch.

> "Once we learn to wait for the Lord's leading in everything, we will know the strength that finds its highest point in an even and steady walk. Waiting—keeping yourself faithful to His leading—is the secret of strength. And anything that does not align with obedience to Him is a waste of time and energy. Watch and wait for His leading." ~ Samuel Dickey Gordon

I will keep watch for You, my strength, because God is my stronghold (Psalm 59:10). "I will stand at my guard post and station myself on the lookout tower. I will watch to see what He will say to me and what I should reply about my complaint. Then the Lord answered me and said, 'Write down the vision and inscribe it clearly on tablets, so that one who reads it may run. For the vision is yet for the appointed time; it hurries toward the goal, and it will not fail. Though it delays, wait for it; for it will certainly come, it will not delay long,'" (Habakkuk 2:1-3).

Allow your heart to entwine with God's heart. Expect, watch, hope in God, and wait on God. Have patience. Take a deep breath. God's timing is always perfect.

> "In God's perfect design for our lives, He has planned for times of fruitfulness and activity. He will also build in times of quiet and rest. There will be times when He asks us to remain faithful, doing the same work day after day. But there will also be periods of excitement and new beginnings. By God's grace, we will enjoy seasons of harvesting and the fruit of our faithfulness. By God's grace, we will also overcome the cold winters of heartache and grief, for without winter there would be no spring. Just as it is with the seasons of nature, these seasons in our lives work together to bring about God's perfect will for each one of us."
> ~ Henry & Richard Blackaby[72]

Therefore, "I wait for the Lord, my soul waits, and in His word do I hope. My soul waits for the Lord more than the watchmen for the morning; Indeed, more than the watchmen for the morning," (Psalm 130:5-6, NASB).

> "The great battle of our spiritual lives is 'Will you believe?' It is squarely a matter of believing God will do what only he can do. That is what God honors. He treasures those who respond and open their hearts to him. He's looking for a faith so strong that it will anchor on his Word and wait for him, the One who makes everything beautiful in its time." ~ Jim Cymbala[73]

Even in the wait, we have the freedom to be still, cease striving, and know that God is God.

God has everything under control. And when the purpose of the waiting is revealed, we'll be left breathless in wonder and awe, praising our amazing God.

Live in the moment

> "The key to the 'with God' life is allowing God to make every moment of our lives glorious with his presence." ~ John Ortberg

What if you gave your children a two-week all-expenses-paid vacation to their favorite location? A loving parent would rejoice when their child enjoyed the gift.

What if the children went on the trip, but their experience was spoiled by the knowledge that it would eventually end?

How often do we forget to enjoy good days because we think a bad day is coming?

God gave us the gift of today, the gift of time. How are we unwrapping His gift?

> "You must arrange your days so that you are experiencing total contentment, joy, and confidence in your everyday life with God—that and that alone is what makes a soul healthy." ~ Dallas Willard

How are we spending and enjoying what God has given?

Fall arrived on the calendar, yet the air remained warm. Trees with their still-green leaves swayed in the wind.

Mesmerized, I sat under a tall oak tree and breathed deep of the beauty of God's nature. The trees' soft swaying drew my gaze upward, toward the heavens and God.

I wonder how many times God waves hope, joy, life, peace, and glory from the heavens?

For many years, the verse in Psalm 94:19 brought comfort. "When my anxious thoughts multiply within me, Your consolations delight my soul."

I read the verse wrong for decades. I thought it was talking about heavenly constellations, getting outside, and seeing the beauty of God's sky.

Hey, it worked for me!

No matter how distracting the world, the enemy, the busyness of life, we can rejoice in God's consolations and His constellations. Step away, step outside, look to the heavens, for God's everlasting loving light always shines.

> "I can see through creation the marvelous fingerprints of God, who is magnificent, awesome, and wonderful." ~ A. W. Tozer

Every day, God is revealing beauty and His tender love.

Flowers dance in the breeze, birds soar on currents of air, and the ocean waves against the shore. Stars twinkle in the night, sparkling and beckoning to the world below, revealing God's grandeur and glory.

Will we live in the moment and take time to notice God's beauty?

> "Live for today, but hold your hands open to tomorrow. Anticipate the future and its changes with joy. There is a seed of God's love in every event, every unpleasant situation in which you may find yourself." ~ Barbara Johnson[74]

One day, while walking and listening to praise music, caught up in the joy of worship, I felt like my hair was standing on end. I even stopped and took a selfie to check. There weren't any outward signs, but what delight as my spirit soared to the heavens. My feet were touching earth, but my soul defied gravity.

We have been brought to life with Christ, and because of our union with Jesus, we are seated in the heavenly places with Him (Ephesians 2:6). If we could truly grasp the truth that our souls live in the heavens, our soul-feet would never touch the ground.

Living in the moment with God, praising and worshiping, filling our thoughts with God's Word and meditating on the goodness of our God, we defy gravity. We walk on air—Holy Spirit air.

> "O, the closest walk with God is the sweetest heaven that can be enjoyed on earth." ~ David Brainerd

Our little dog sleeps in her crate. Come morning, her excitement bubbles over as we release her. Her tail, a blur of fur, whips back and forth with the force of helicopter blades. She never fails to be happy to see us. We know she loves us.

How often do we wake in the morning and tell God we love Him?

How often do we show our appreciation and love to the One who loves us most?

> "Certainty is the mark of the commonsense life—gracious uncertainty is the mark of the spiritual life. To be certain of God means that we are uncertain in all our ways, not knowing what tomorrow may bring. This is generally expressed with a sigh of sadness, but it should be an expression of breathless expectation. We are uncertain of the next step, but we are certain of God."
> ~ Oswald Chambers[75]

Regardless of the uncertainty of the future, imagine how different life would be if we met every day with a breathless expectation of what God would do?

God's ways and His plans are so much more than we can imagine.

God loves you. His grace is for you.

Finding Freedom in a Binding World

Trust God and step out into the freedom of breathless expectation.

Lisa Buffaloe

Glow and shine

A sports drink commercial shows athletes' skin glowing with its product. Their logo says, "Is it in you?"

Is Christ in you?

What do people see when they look at us? Are we radiating and beaming with Christ?

> "People are like stained-glass windows. They sparkle and shine when the sun is out, but when the darkness sets in, their true beauty is revealed only if there is a light from within."
> ~ Elisabeth Kubler-Ross

Psalm 34:5 tells us that when we look to God, our faces radiate with joy. Moses's face shone after talking with God, so much so that he had to wear a veil over his face (Exodus 34:29-33).

Stephen was a Godly man, and even his face revealed that fact. Stephen glowed with God (Acts 6:15).

Missionary Adoniram Judson beamed for Christ so much that one little boy said he had never seen such a light on any human face, and others called Mr. Judson, "Mr. Glory-face."

Another Christian man was described as having his face radiate gratitude for past blessings and love for everyone.

Do you glow with Christ?

If we live in God's love, we will radiate God's love because we radiate what is inside.

Jesus said His disciples are "the light of the world" (Matthew 5:14). In the world's darkness, Christians are to be beacons of light, bearers of The Good News shining Christ in the dark world.

> "Just as the lampstand has been strategically and purposefully placed in the Holy Place, you have been strategically and purposefully placed in the world to shine Christ for his glory."
> ~ Shawn Barnard

Lighthouses were constructed to help ship captains avoid hazardous coastal areas and navigate safely into ports. Despite differences in size, shape, and color, each structure held lights that guide sailors to safety. In the night's darkness, the light is visible.

Many are perishing and in need of the light of Christ.

> "A man at sea was once very seasick. He heard that a man had fallen overboard. He couldn't do much, but he laid hold of a light and held it up to the porthole. The light fell on the drowning man's hand, and a man caught him and pulled him into the lifeboat. It seemed a small thing to do to hold up the light; yet it saved the man's life. We can do as much as that. If we cannot do some great thing, we can hold the light for some poor, perishing soul, who is out in the dark waters of sin." ~ D L Moody

Jesus promises that those who believe in Him will find the light of life and will never be in darkness (John 8:12). Therefore, arise, shine; for your light has come, and the glory of the Lord has risen upon you (Isaiah 60:1).

Glow in Christ and glow for Christ.

As Christians, we reflect the Lord's glory and are being transformed into his likeness with ever-increasing glory. God used the good news to call you to be saved so you can share in the glory of our Lord Jesus Christ. Those whom he predestined he also called, and those whom he called he also justified, and those whom he justified he also glorified (2 Corinthians 3:18, 2 Thessalonians 2:14, Romans 8:30).

You are here to proclaim the excellencies of Him who has called you out of darkness into His marvelous light (1 Peter 2:9).

Therefore, "Let your light so shine before men, that they may see your good works and glorify your Father in heaven. Here's another way to put it: You're here to be light, bringing out the God-colors in the world. God is not a secret to be kept. We're going public with this, as public as a city on a hill. If I make you light-bearers, you don't think I'm going to hide you under a bucket, do you? I'm putting you on a light stand. Now that I've put you there on a hilltop, on a light stand—shine!" (Matthew 5:16, NKJV, Matthew 5:14-15, MSG).

Allow your light to shine with God's freedom and love, so that others may see the light of Christ.

Be an encourager

In the 1996 Olympics, Gymnast Kerri Strug injured her ankle. In great pain, she gave an incredible performance on her vault routine, and the United States won gold.

Kerri was asked how she had accomplished such a feat. Even in pain, she said she focused on her coach, who kept telling her she could do it and reminding her of what was at stake. His words of support and encouragement spurred her on to victory.

Years ago, I noticed a little hurt sparrow fluttering on the ground. Several birds gathered around him, chirping, nudging, and cheering him on. The little sparrow continued to struggle, and then, because of their encouragement, he regained his strength and flew away.

What if we were like those small birds, offering support to those who falter, encouraging, and offering a gentle touch to those in need?

> "Every human being you know is making a request of their friends, though it usually goes unspoken. Here's what they ask: 'Motivate me. Call out the best in me. Believe in me. Encourage me when I'm tempted to quit. Speak truth to me and remind me of my deepest values. Help me achieve my greatest potential. Tell me again what God called me to be, what I might yet become.'" ~ John Ortberg[76]

When God lays a name on your heart, act in prayer, share encouraging scripture, take time to visit, send a note, text, or email.

Pray for guidance on how best to pray and minister to others, for only the Lord knows what is truly needed.

> "We can never untangle all the woes in other people's lives. We can't produce miracles overnight. But we can bring a cup of cool water to a thirsty soul, or a scoop of laughter to a lonely heart."
> ~ Barbara Johnson[77]

According to Hebrews 10:24-25, we should be considerate and supportive of each other by demonstrating love, engaging in good deeds, gathering together, and offering encouragement.

> "One of the highest of human duties is the duty of encouragement. It is easy to laugh at men's ideas; it is easy to pour cold water on their enthusiasm; it is easy to discourage others. The world is full of discouragers. We have a Christian duty to encourage one another. Many a time, a word of praise or thanks or appreciation or cheer has kept a man on his feet. Blessed is the man [or woman] who speaks such a word." ~ William Barclay

Let's be like Barnabas. Acts 11:23 tells us he was known as the son of encouragement. Not only that, Barnabas was a man full of joy, encouraging early Christians to remain faithful and devoted to the Lord.

Barnabas knew the gift of encouragement and that the path to blessings often lies in blessing others.

Encouragement is the action of giving someone support, confidence, or hope. Encouragement also brings courage.

As we encourage others, we strengthen them and are encouraged in return.

> "Don't let your life speed out of control. Live intentionally. Do something today that will last beyond your lifetime."
> ~ Barbara Johnson

Live with purpose.

> "You can encourage someone with a word. You can give a flower to someone. You can do something. When you do, Jesus will open the door for you for more. Take the step." ~ Mama Maggie

"Therefore encourage (admonish, exhort) one another and edify (strengthen and build up) one another," (1 Thessalonians 5:11, AMPC).

> "We can never untangle all the woes in other people's lives. We can't produce miracles overnight. But we can bring a cup of cool water to a thirsty soul, or a scoop of laughter to a lonely heart."
> ~ Barbara Johnson[78]

In a world bound by trouble and heartache, encouragement matters. Help untangle lives, and you will be blessed. "Give away your life; you'll find life given back, but not merely given back—given back with bonus and blessing. Giving, not getting, is the way. Generosity begets generosity," (Luke 6:37-38, MSG).

.

Lisa Buffaloe

Share the good news

I once had the privilege of interviewing a missionary whose method of spreading the gospel in the Colombian jungle involved dropping packages from airplanes. The parcels, bundled under small parachutes, contained Bibles, Christian literature, and films, as well as radios pre-set to Christian stations.

Imagine the joy of those living in remote areas when they discovered the gifts and heard the good news about Jesus Christ.

> "There are lots of stories in the Bible, but all the stories are telling one Big Story. The Story of how God loves his children and comes to rescue them." ~ Sally Lloyd-Jones[79]

Why do we hesitate to share God's wonderful news?

Jesus Christ set us free; let's remember to use our freedom to show others the way to theirs.

> "Deep within my soul, I was moved to feel compassion for perishing sinners and for a world lulled to sleep by the wicked Enemy. And I began to think, 'Should I not do whatever I can for the Lord Jesus and try to awake His slumbering church before He returns?'" ~ George Mueller[80]

When someone embraces Jesus as Lord and Savior, they are given freedom from the burden of sin and gain fellowship with God, Jesus, the Holy Spirit, and other Christians.

Jesus instructed His disciples to go and make disciples of all nations (Matthew 28:18-20). After Jesus set a man free from a legion of demons, He told the man to tell others what God had done for him (Mark 5:1-20).

Has Christ set you free? Will you share the good news of what Christ has done for you?

> "I want to be the kind of person who shows the love of Christ in such a dynamic way that I will be creating in their hearts a thirst for God." ~ A. W. Tozer

Oh, may that be true of us!

Are we moved to compassion for those who don't know Jesus Christ as Savior?

According to Acts 2, Peter, bold with courage, told a crowd that Jesus had been delivered up according to the definite plan and foreknowledge of God, crucified and killed by the hands of lawless men. Many of those people listening had been the very ones who demanded the crucifixion of Jesus.

It would have been easier for Peter to talk only about God's love. Yet Peter loved God enough, and loved others enough, to speak the truth.

The truth is often difficult to hear, but the truth sets free.

Peter spoke the truth, and when the crowd heard, "they were cut to the heart" and asked what they could do to be saved. Peter told them to repent and be baptized in the name of Jesus Christ for the forgiveness of their sins, and to receive the gift of the Holy Spirit (Acts 2:37).

As the truth is proclaimed, the Holy Spirit works to touch the hearts of those who hear, revealing, broadening understanding, and motivating listeners to abandon sin and find salvation.

Our love for God and for others needs to be more than making someone comfortable. Our love needs to be strong enough to speak the truth.

Speaking God's Word, the Truth will make a difference and have an impact, for the word of God is living and active, sharper than any two-edged sword, piercing to the division of soul and of spirit, of joints and of marrow, and discerning the thoughts and intentions of the heart (Hebrews 4:12). God's word sprouts, grows, never returns empty, and accomplishes all that God desires (Isaiah 55:10-11).

The apostle Paul took advantage of every day and every experience, including his trials, as opportunities to share the gospel of Christ. He even spread the good news while being chained between two guards.

> "There are two sides to every chain. He (Paul) didn't look at the situation and go, 'I'm chained to this guard.' He looked and said, 'The guard is chained to me. He can't go anywhere.'"
> ~ Levi Lusko

While undergoing cancer treatments, one of my Christian author friends shared eighty-two copies of his books with nurses, doctors, and patients. Another friend who suffered from pancreatic cancer shared with everyone she met about Christ

Please don't let Satan convince you that you can't make an impact for God. In our world, numbers gauge success, yet with God, every soul mattered so much to God that He sent His one and only Son. Everyone matters to God, and every one of your acts of service will matter to God.

Because of the faith of one woman, Rahab, she and her family were spared.

Because of the faith of one man, Daniel, a nation turned to God.

Because of the faith of one man, Nehemiah, a wall was built.

Because of one Savior, the world is offered salvation.

Because of the One who lives within you, nothing is impossible.

God looks for ones who fear Him, who are faithful to Him, who are righteous, who walk with Him, and will minister in His name, for the eyes of the Lord move throughout the earth to find the ones whose hearts are completely His that He may strongly support them (2 Chronicles 16:9).

If Christ lives in you, the power of God Himself is also within you. Trust God; let Him use you for His excellent, extraordinary plans.

> "All of God's people are ordinary people who have been made extraordinary by the purpose He has given them."
> ~ Oswald Chambers

Spread the good news. Tell others about Jesus, "to open their eyes, so they may turn from darkness to light and from the power of Satan to God. Then they will receive forgiveness for their sins and be given a place among God's people, who are set apart by faith in Christ," (Acts 26:18, NLT).

In your freedom in Christ, share the good news of the freedom given by our amazing Savior and God.

You'll get safely through

In Acts 18:1, Luke wrote, "After we were brought safely through." The interesting thing is that Luke, Paul, and everyone on that ship had just experienced a horrible storm and shipwreck.

Most people would not say they had been "brought safely through," they would probably focus on the terrible time they encountered while being in a raging sea for days and days, that the ship's cargo was lost, and the boat was destroyed.

Paul had years of mistreatment. He was beaten, stoned, jailed, people repeatedly tried to kill him, he lived through several shipwrecks, and he experienced hardships and trials beyond what most people could endure.

However, Paul did not sit around feeling sorry for himself, whining and complaining about his numerous difficulties. He maintained a proper perspective by keeping his focus on Christ.

What if we did the same? Regardless of how painful our journey, what if we continued to trust God?

A car salesman got the ride of his life when racecar driver Jeff Gordon, in disguise as an older gentleman, visited his dealership for a test drive. Jeff did not hold back as he drove off the lot and onto the streets.

Finding Freedom in a Binding World

During the crazy, high-speed test drive, the poor car sales agent was terrified and screamed in horror the entire time.

When Jeff returned to the dealership, the salesman jumped out of the car, ready to call the police and report Jeff.

Yet when Jeff identified himself, the man's face showed relief, then delight as he realized a famous, highly skilled racecar driver had been in control all along. The man quickly asked, "Want to do it again?"

God is in control; you can trust Him. No matter how rough life's ride may be, with Christ Jesus in the driver's seat, you will be brought safely through.

> "When Thou passest through the waters, deep the waves may be and cold, but JEHOVAH is our Refuge and His promise is our hold. For the LORD Himself hath said it, He the faithful God and true. When thou comest to the waters, thou shalt not go down, but through. Seas of sorrow, seas of trial, bitterest anguish, fiercest pain, rolling surges of temptation, sweeping over heart and brain, they shall never overflow us, for we know His word is true. All His waves and all His billows He will lead us safely through. Threatening breakers of destruction, doubt's insidious undertow, shall not sink us, shall not drag us out to ocean depths of woe. For His promise shall sustain us, praise the LORD, whose word is true! We shall not go down or under. He hath said, "Thou passest through." ~ Annie Johnson Flint

Buckle in. Life's ride may be wild, hair-raising, and crazy, but God will get you through every trial and difficulty. His love, power, wisdom, and strength are in the driver's seat, and He will get you safely through.

The joyful end

Paul wrote always to be full of joy, always rejoicing, and to rejoice in the Lord always. James said to count it all joy during our trials.

With all the problems in the world, how on earth do we do that?

Perhaps being joyful is possible when we remember that genuine joy isn't earthbound. Divine joy is constant, continuously flowing from God's throne.

> "The secret of joy is always a matter of focus: a resolute focusing on the Father, not on the fears. All fear is but the notion that God's love ends. *When does He ever end?* When you can't touch bottom, is when you touch the depths of God." ~ Ann Voskamp[81]

The boundless love of God is immeasurable. In God's presence is fullness of joy; honor and majesty are found in His presence; strength and joy are found in His sanctuary. And the joy of the Lord is our strength (Psalm 16:11, 1 Chronicles 16:27, Nehemiah 8:10).

We can rejoice because God is our Father and has given us a connection with Him through His Son, Jesus Christ. Joy comes from knowing Christ knows our every imperfection, flaw, failure, and sin, and still loves us, forgives, and washes us clean. His joy and delight will be in us, full and complete and overflowing (John 15:11).

Even when troubles arise, we can rejoice that Jesus has conquered and overcome the world, and nothing is impossible for Him to help us conquer or overcome.

> "Joy is a choice. It is a matter of attitude that stems from one's confidence in God—that He is at work, that He is in full control, that He is in the midst of whatever has happened, is happening, and will happen." ~ Charles R. Swindoll

Our actions or inaction do not hinder God's joy. Even when our mood changes, God's joy remains.

> "Life is a refining process. Our response to it determines whether we'll be ground down or polished up. On a piano, one person sits down and plays sonatas, while another merely bangs away at "Chopsticks." The piano is not responsible. It's how you touch the keys that makes the difference. It's how you play what life gives you that determines your joy and shine." ~ Barbara Johnson[82]

Difficulties and unplanned circumstances will come our way, yet we have a choice in how we respond. Choose joy. Even in life's difficulties, fight back with defiant joy, for your Heavenly Father's love is unending.

> "Practicing defiant joy is the declaration that the darkness does not and will not win. When we fight back with joy, we embrace a reality that is more real than what we're enduring, and we awaken to the deepest reality of our identity as beloved, joyful children of God." ~ Margaret Feinberg

Do you know what else we can celebrate?

The joyful end is coming.

The tomb couldn't contain our Savior, and it won't contain us either!

Jesus died and rose from the grave, and God will bring back to life those who died in Jesus (1 Thessalonians 4:14).

> "Heaven is not the best the world has to offer. Heaven is the best God has to offer. Heaven is the place of supreme beauty because perfection is there. The perfect God, the God of unqualified beauty — He is there, and heaven is going to be beautiful."
> ~ A. W. Tozer[83]

For those who love Christ, death is never a punishment.

> "Why do we think of death as something wholly apart from God? Has not the Lord a right to send for those whom He will, for those who are ready, for those whose time upon earth must come to an end? Death is a necessity. Death is servant, not master. And there is a final great day coming when 'Death is swallowed up in victory; (1 Corinthians 15:54 NKJV). Men do not die when Christ is in the house; they ascend." ~ Joseph Parker [84]

We can't even imagine the beauty of heaven, where joy will be experienced throughout eternity.

"Things which eye has not seen and ear has not heard, and which have not entered the human heart, all that God has prepared for those who love Him," (1 Corinthians 2:9, NASB). That verse also implies that God has wonderful things planned for those who love Him at this very moment.

> "Your place in heaven will seem to be made for you and you alone, because you were made for it—made for it stitch by stitch as a glove is made for a hand." ~ C.S. Lewis[85]

Once we shed off our earthly flesh suits, we live forever in a new body that never decays, where pain doesn't exist, and tears are only shed in pure joy and delight.

Death is not the end.

When Missionary Amy Carmichael was told she might not have many years left, she was elated.

In Amy's journal, she wrote that death was a blissful thing and purest golden joy. She knew that death leads to the end of the heartache of this world to step into paradise and the unending joy of eternity with God.

> "Death is no punishment to the believer: it is the gate of endless joy." - Charles Spurgeon

If Christ is your Savior, your ending will be incredible!

God will wipe away every tear from their eyes; and there will no longer be any death; there will no longer be any mourning, or crying, or pain; the first things have passed away. God, who sits on the throne, is making all things new (Revelation 21:4-5).

Your amazing end is coming.

Until then, keep focused on God, care for your soul, spend time with God, tame your thoughts, be courageous through difficulties, keep moving forward.

And when your Heavenly room is ready, the Lord will guide you to your blissful eternity in Heaven.

One last note

"Mark well that if the Son of God shall make you free, you shall be free indeed, and in that freedom find life sparkling, flashing, and overflowing like the streams of a fountain. Pray to Jesus to make you all you can be. Say to Him, 'Use me to the fullness of my capability. Touch my silent tongue, equip my idle hands, and open my frostbitten wallet. Send a full stream of life upon me that all my soul may wake up, and all that is within me may adore you. Get out of me all that can possibly come out of such a poor thing as I am. Let your Spirit work in me to the praise of the glory of your grace.' Oh, for men and women who are alive from head to foot, whose entire existence is full of consecration to Jesus and zeal for the divine glory; these have life 'to the full" ~ Charles Spurgeon

"Tell God that He has the freedom to do anything He has to do to lead you to complete freedom." ~ T. W. Hunt

Live in God's freedom and go, make disciples of all the nations, baptizing them in the name of the Father and of the Son and of the Holy Spirit, teaching them to observe all things that Jesus commanded; for He is with you always, even to the end of the age (Matthew 28:19-20).

About the Author

Lisa Buffaloe is a happily married mom, speaker, and multi-published author. She loves spending time with God, her sweet hubby, studying the Bible, writing, and enjoying nature.

Please visit Lisa at https://lisabuffaloe.com
Facebook https://facebook.com/lisabuffaloe
Twitter (X) https://x.com/lisabuffaloe
Instagram https://instagram.com/buffaloelisa
Amazon https://amzn.to/4ltfEBA

Books by Lisa

Fiction

Crawdad Beach Series
Each book may be enjoyed separately or as part of the series.

Visible, yet Hidden
Running to Grace
Crystal's Journey Home
A Baker's Heart
Stella's Heart Code
River Steps Free
Mia Lets Go
A New Paige
Running from Shame
Elise's New Song
A Found Joy
A Healing Rain

Hope and Grace Series
Each book may be enjoyed separately or as part of the series.

Nadia's Hope
Prodigal Nights
Writing Her Heart
The Discovery Chapter
Open Lens

Stand-alone novels

The Masterpiece Beneath
The Fortune
Grace for the Char-Baked

Non-Fiction

Finding Freedom in a Binding World
Float by Faith
Heart and Soul Medication
Time with The Timeless One
The Forgotten Resting Place
Present in His Presence
We Were Meant for Paradise
One Lit Step: Devotions for your journey
The Unnamed Devotional
Flying on His Wings
Unfailing Treasures
No Wound Too Deep For The Deep Love of Christ
Living Joyfully Free Devotional (Volumes 1 & 2)

Acknowledgments

There are not sufficient words in my vocabulary to thank God adequately for who He is, and all He has done. Despite the times I ran from Him in disobedience, He lovingly sought me, offering forgiveness and grace-filled mercy. Through the pain, He has held me close. Through the highs and lows of life, His love has been my constant support.

Heavenly Father, thank You for all You have done and all You will do in the future. Thank You for Your presence. I am so thankful for Your everlasting love and the amazing freedom You offer and give. May this book honor You.

Thank you, Dennis, for being a loving, wonderful husband. Thank you for your prayers, support, and encouragement. I love you!

Thank you to the authors who have shared wisdom.

Patricia (Pacjac) Carroll, thank you again for your helpful feedback.

Readers, thank you for taking the time to read *Finding Freedom in a Binding World*.

If you enjoyed the book, would you be so kind as to please write a favorable review and recommend it to others? Thank you.

Visit my Amazon page @ .https://amzn.to/48REJ5O

Bible Credits and Bibliography

The original text of the Bible is rich and full, written in Hebrew, Aramaic, and Greek. The various Bible versions used are intended to share the one that best reveals the beauty and truth of each verse. Some verses are repeated to press home the timeless truth of God's word.

I gratefully thank each Bible publisher for the use of the scripture quotations.

Scripture taken from the New Century Version® (NCV). Copyright © 2005 by Thomas Nelson, Inc. Used by permission. All rights reserved.

Living Bible (TLB) The Living Bible copyright © 1971 by Tyndale House Foundation. Used by permission of Tyndale House Publishers Inc., Carol Stream, Illinois 60188. All rights reserved.

Scripture quotations taken from the New American Standard Bible®, NASB, Copyright © 1960, 1962, 1963, 1968, 1971, 1972, 1973, 1975, 1977, 1995 by The Lockman Foundation Used by permission. www.Lockman.org

Scripture quotations marked (NLT) are taken from the Holy Bible, New Living Translation, copyright © 1996, 2004, 2007 by Tyndale House Foundation, used by permission of Tyndale House Publishers, Inc., Carol Stream, Illinois 60188. All rights reserved.

NET Bible® copyright ©1996-2006 by Biblical Studies Press, L.L.C. http://netbible.com

Scripture taken from the New King James Version®. Copyright © 1982 by Thomas Nelson, Inc. Used by permission. All rights reserved.

New American Standard Bible 1995 (NASB1995), New American Standard Bible®, Copyright © 1960, 1971, 1977, 1995 by The Lockman Foundation. All rights reserved.

The ESV® Bible (The Holy Bible, English Standard Version®). ESV® Text Edition: 2016. Copyright © 2001 by Crossway, a publishing ministry of Good News Publishers. The ESV® text has been reproduced in cooperation with and by permission of Good News Publishers.

Scripture taken from The Message. Copyright © 1993, 1994, 1995, 1996, 2000, 2001, 2002. Used by permission of NavPress Publishing Group.

Scripture quotations taken from the Amplified® Bible (AMP), Copyright © 2015 by The Lockman Foundation Used by permission. www.Lockman.org

Scripture quotations taken from the Amplified® Bible (AMPC), Copyright © 1954, 1958, 1962, 1964, 1965, 1987 by The Lockman Foundation Used by permission. www.Lockman.org

Holman Christian Standard Bible (HCSB) Copyright © 1999, 2000, 2002, 2003, 2009 by Holman Bible Publishers, Nashville, Tennessee. All rights reserved.

The Passion Translation®. (TPT) Copyright © 2017 by BroadStreet Publishing® Group, LLC. Used by permission. All rights reserved. ThePassionTranslation.com

---

[1] S. D. Gordon, *Quiet Talk on John's Gospel*, Compiled by Lance Wubbels, Bethany House, Bloomington, MN
[2] A. W. Tozer, *No Greater Love*, Bethany House, Minneapolis, MN
[3] Charles Allen, *All Things Are Possible Through Prayer*, Revell
[4] A. W. Tozer, *Delighting in God*, compiled and edited by James L. Snyder, Bethany House, 2015
[5] Madam Guyon, *Letters of Madam Guyon*
[6] J. R. Miller, *Making the Most of Life*
[7] Charles Spurgeon, *Morning and Evening*, revised and updated by Alistair Begg. Copyright © 2003, Crossway, a publishing ministry of Good News Publishers, Wheaton, IL 6018
[8] Henry and Richard Blackaby, Claude King, *7 Truths from Experiencing God*, LifeWay Press, Nashville, TN
[9] Dallas Willard as quoted in *Soul Keeping* by John Ortberg, Zondervan, Grand Rapids, MI, 2014
[10] Mark Buchanan, *The Rest of God: Restoring Your Soul by Restoring Sabbath*, Thomas Nelson, Nashville, TN
[11] John Ortberg, *Soul Keeping*, Zondervan, Grand Rapids, MI, 2014
[12] Joanna Weaver, *Embracing Trust: The Art of Letting Go and Holding On to a Forever-Faithful God*, Revell, Baker Publishing Group, Ada, MI
[13] Ann Voskamp, *One Thousand Gifts: A Dare to Live Fully Right Where You Are*, Zondervan
[14] A. W. Tozer, *No Greater Love*, Bethany House, Minneapolis, MN

15 A. W. Tozer, *No Greater Love*, Bethany House, Minneapolis, MN
16 Henry Cloud, *False Assumptions - Relief From 12 'Christian' Beliefs that can drive you crazy*, Zondervan
17 Margaret Feinberg, *Fight Back With Joy*, Worthy Publishing, Brentwood, TN
18 Weaver, Joanna, *Embracing Trust: The Art of Letting Go and Holding On to a Forever-Faithful God*, Revell, Grand Rapids, MI
19 Rob Currie, *Hungry for More of God*, AMG Publishers
20 Janet Perez Eckles, *Now I see*, JC Empowerment Ministries, 2023
21 Sharon Jaynes, *Take Hold of the Faith You Long For: Let Go, Move Forward, Live Bold*, Baker Books
22 Sharon Jaynes, Gwen Smith, Mary Southerland, *Knowing God by Name*, Multnomah
23 Sharon Jaynes, *Take Hold Of The Faith You Long Fo*
24 Gwen Smith, *Broken into Beautiful*, Harvest House Publishers, Eugene, OR, 2008
25 Jim Cymbala, *Fresh Faith: What Happens When Real Faith Ignites God's People*, Zondervan
26 John Ortberg, *Water-Walking*, Zondervan, Grand Rapids, MI, 2019
27 Sharon Jaynes, *The Power of a Woman's Words*, Harvest House Publishers, 2007
28 Oswald Chambers, *My Utmost for His Highest*
29 A. W. Tozer, *Delighting in God*, compiled and edited by James L. Snyder, Bethany House
30 L. B. Cowman, *Streams in the Desert*, Grand Rapids, MI: Zondervan
31 Allen Arnold, https://www.withallen.com/blog/trust-the-storyteller
32 Lettie Cowman, *Streams in the Desert*, Grand Rapids, MI
33 Mark Buchanan, *The Rest of God*
34 Robert Morgan, *The Red Sea Rules: 10 God-Given Strategies for Difficult Times*, Zondervan
35 L. B. Cowman, *Streams in the Desert*, Grand Rapids, MI: Zondervan
36 John Ortberg, *Everybody's Normal Till You Get to Know Them*, Zondervan
37 Jill Briscoe, *Faith Enough to Finish*, Tyndale
38 Helen Roseveare, *Living Fellowship: Willing to be the third side of the triangle*, Christian Focus Publications, Scotland, UK
39 Helen Roseveare, *Living Fellowship: Willing to be the third side of the triangle*
40 Helen Roseveare, *Living Fellowship: Willing to be the third side of the triangle*
41 Amy Carmichael, *,Edges of His Ways*, Dohnavur Fellowship, 1975
42 Gwen Smith, *I Want It All*, David C. Cook Colorado Springs, CO, 2016
43 Amy Carmichael, *Candles in the Dark*, CLC Publications, Fort Washington, PA
44 Helen Roseveare, *Living Holiness: Willing to be the Legs of a Galloping Horse*, Christian Focus Publications, Scotland, UK
45 L. B. Cowman, *Streams in the Desert*, Grand Rapids, MI
46 Dr. Helen Roseveare, *Give Me this Mountain*, Christian Focus Publications, Scotland, UK
47 Cowman, L. B., *Streams In The Desert*, Grand Rapids, MI: Zondervan
48 Anne Graham Lotz, *Why? Trusting God When You Don't Understand*, W Publishing Group, 2007

[49] Leslie Ginevra Montgomery (used by permission) https://www.facebook.com/LeslieGinevraMontgomery
[50] Leslie Ginevra Montgomery (used by permission) https://www.facebook.com/LeslieGinevraMontgomery
[51] L. B. Cowman, *Streams In The Desert*
[52] Joni Eareckson Tada, *A Place of Healing: Wrestling with the Mysteries of Suffering, Pain, and God's Sovereignty*
[53] Henry and Richard Blackaby, *Experiencing God Day-by-Day*
[54] Gwen Smith, https://gwensmith.net/choosing-to-trust-god-2/
[55] A. W. Tozer, *Delighting in God*, compiled and edited by James L. Snyder, Bethany House, 2015
[56] Barbara Johnson, *Boomerang Joy: Joy That Goes Around, Comes Around*, Zondervan
[57] Henry & Richard Blackaby, *Experiencing God Day-by-Day*: The Devotional and Journal
[58] Willard, Dallas, *The Great Omission: Reclaiming Jesus's Essential Teachings on Discipleship*. Copyright © 2006 HarperCollins Publishers.
[59] Sharon Jaynes, *Take Hold of the Faith You Long for*, 2016 Baker Books
[60] John Ortberg, *Water-Walking: Discovering and Obeying Your Call to Radical Discipleship*, Zondervan
[61] Ann Voskamp, https://annvoskamp.com/
[62] Elisabeth Elliot, *Secure in the Everlasting Arms: Trusting the God Who Never Leaves Your Side*, Revell
[63] Warren W. Wiersbe, *New Testament Words for Today: 100 Devotional Reflections*, Baker Books, 2013
[64] Henry & Richard Blackaby, *Experiencing God Day-by-Day*
[65] *Living Holiness: Willing to be the Legs of a Galloping Horse*
[66] Compiled and edited by Lance Wubbels, *Day by day through the Gospel of John*, Bethany House, 2018
[67] Henry & Richard Blackaby, *Experiencing God Day-by-Day*
[68] Oswald Chambers, *My Utmost for His Highest*
[69] Luci Swindoll, *The Joyful Journey*, Zondervan Publishing House, Grand Rapids, Michigan,
[70] John Ortberg, *Soul Keeping: Caring for the Most Important Part of You*,, Zondervan, Grand Rapids, MI, 2014
[71] Warren Wiersbe, *The Bumps Are What You Climb On*
[72] Henry & Richard Blackaby, *Experiencing God Day-by-Day*
[73] Jim Cymbala *Fresh Faith*
[74] Barbara Johnson, *Boomerang Joy: Joy That Goes Around, Comes Around*, Zondervan (2000).
[75] Oswald Chambers, *My Utmost for His Highest*
[76] John Ortberg, *Everybody's Normal Till You Get to Know Them*, Zondervan
[77] Barbara Johnson, *Boomerang Joy: Joy That Goes Around, Comes Around*, Zondervan
[78] Barbara Johnson, *Boomerang Joy: Joy That Goes Around, Comes Around*, Zondervan
[79] Sally Lloyd-Jones, *The Jesus Storybook Bible*, Zonderkids
[80] L. B. Cowman, *Streams In The Desert*, Zondervan, Grand Rapids, MI
[81] Ann Voskamp, *The Greatest Gift*
[82] Barbara Johnson, *Boomerang Joy: Joy That Goes Around, Comes Around*,

Zondervan (2000).
[83] A. W. Tozer, *Delighting in God*, compiled and edited by James L. Snyder, Bethany House, 2015
[84] *Day by Day Through the Gospel of John*, July 8
[85] C.S. Lewis, *Made for Heaven*, Harper San Francisco, p 21-23

Thank you for reading,

Finding Freedom in a Binding World

Lisa Buffaloe

www.ingramcontent.com/pod-product-compliance
Lightning Source LLC
Chambersburg PA
CBHW061328040426
42444CB00011B/2819